# LOST CANYON

## A STORY OF LOSS
## A JOURNEY OF HEALING

### SEAN M. FLEMING

Lost Canyon

Sean M. Fleming

© Copyright 2012 Sean M. Fleming

All rights reserved.

No part of this book may be reproduced or transmitted in any form by any means, electronic or mechanical, including photocopying, recording or by any information storage and retrieval system, without specific written permission from the publisher. The scanning, uploading, and distribution of this book via the Internet or via any other means without the permission of the publisher is illegal and punishable by law. Please purchase only authorized electronic editions, and do not participate in or encourage electronic piracy of copyrighted materials.

Cover Design by Wesley Bryant

Library of Congress Cataloging-in-Publication Data Pending

Sean M. Fleming

Lost Canyon /Fleming, Sean M.

Library of Congress Control Number: 2012910962

ISBN 978-1-60645-098-7 soft cover

ISBN 978-1-60645-099-4 eBook

FIRST PRINTING

10 9 8 7 6 5 4 3 2 1

# TABLE OF CONTENTS

Acknowledgments . . . . . . . . . . . . . . . . . . . . . . . . . . . . .5
Introduction
    Doubts are Traitors . . . . . . . . . . . . . . . . . . . . . . . . . 7

## LOSS

The Dragonfly . . . . . . . . . . . . . . . . . . . . . . . . . . . . . .15
Lost Canyon . . . . . . . . . . . . . . . . . . . . . . . . . . . . . . 23
The Beginning . . . . . . . . . . . . . . . . . . . . . . . . . . . . . 31
A "Perfect" Family . . . . . . . . . . . . . . . . . . . . . . . . . . . .37
Prelude to Broken Hearts . . . . . . . . . . . . . . . . . . . . . . 43
The Phone Call . . . . . . . . . . . . . . . . . . . . . . . . . . . . 49
Canyon Grieves with Grandma . . . . . . . . . . . . . . . . . . . .59
    The Letter . . . . . . . . . . . . . . . . . . . . . . . . . . . . . . 62
The Silent Door . . . . . . . . . . . . . . . . . . . . . . . . . . . . 65
Dandelions in the Outfield . . . . . . . . . . . . . . . . . . . . . .71
Little Things . . . . . . . . . . . . . . . . . . . . . . . . . . . . . . .75
Red-Shell Sand . . . . . . . . . . . . . . . . . . . . . . . . . . . . 83
The Accident . . . . . . . . . . . . . . . . . . . . . . . . . . . . . . .91
    Twenty-Two Years Earlier . . . . . . . . . . . . . . . . . . . . . 93
The Unquenchable Question . . . . . . . . . . . . . . . . . . . . . 95

## GRIEVING

Premonitions . . . . . . . . . . . . . . . . . . . . . . . . . . . . . . 101
Roller Coaster of Emotions . . . . . . . . . . . . . . . . . . . . . 105
    Anger . . . . . . . . . . . . . . . . . . . . . . . . . . . . . . . . . 106
    Sadness . . . . . . . . . . . . . . . . . . . . . . . . . . . . . . . . 108
    Fear . . . . . . . . . . . . . . . . . . . . . . . . . . . . . . . . . . 109
    Guilt . . . . . . . . . . . . . . . . . . . . . . . . . . . . . . . . . . 111

Running on Empty . . . . . . . . . . . . . . . . . . . . . . . . . . . . . . 113
Sleepless night . . . . . . . . . . . . . . . . . . . . . . . . . . . . . . . 123
Sorrow Comes in Waves . . . . . . . . . . . . . . . . . . . . . . . . 129
Grieving. . . . . . . . . . . . . . . . . . . . . . . . . . . . . . . . . . . . 135
The Void. . . . . . . . . . . . . . . . . . . . . . . . . . . . . . . . . . . 141
The Merit of Distraction . . . . . . . . . . . . . . . . . . . . . . . 147
Marriage after Death . . . . . . . . . . . . . . . . . . . . . . . . . . 151
Can I Change the Stars? . . . . . . . . . . . . . . . . . . . . . . . 159
   The Silver Apprentice . . . . . . . . . . . . . . . . . . . . . . . . 161

## HEALING

The Ripples of a Fumble . . . . . . . . . . . . . . . . . . . . . . . 167
Moments of Regret. . . . . . . . . . . . . . . . . . . . . . . . . . . 171
   History Repeats Itself . . . . . . . . . . . . . . . . . . . . . . . . 175
A Lesson from Eddie . . . . . . . . . . . . . . . . . . . . . . . . . 179
A Key Called Forgiveness . . . . . . . . . . . . . . . . . . . . . . 183
Love Leavens. . . . . . . . . . . . . . . . . . . . . . . . . . . . . . . 189
Fort Building & Courage. . . . . . . . . . . . . . . . . . . . . . . 195
   Courage Scores Big. . . . . . . . . . . . . . . . . . . . . . . . . . 197
   Faith and Courage . . . . . . . . . . . . . . . . . . . . . . . . . . 205
Gratitude - A Master Key . . . . . . . . . . . . . . . . . . . . . . 207
My Red-Shell Treasures . . . . . . . . . . . . . . . . . . . . . . . 217
Return to Lost Canyon. . . . . . . . . . . . . . . . . . . . . . . . 221
   Finding Lost Canyon. . . . . . . . . . . . . . . . . . . . . . . . . 229

About the Author . . . . . . . . . . . . . . . . . . . . . . . . . . . 233

# ACKNOWLEDGMENTS

*"Forgiveness is the key that unlocks the door of eternity, and helps me become who I am meant to be."*

~ Sean M. Fleming

I DEDICATE THIS BOOK TO MY SON, CANYON. Thank you for teaching me that I can patiently wait until the day you greet me on distant shores. You taught me values I might not have learned without facing the painful reality of losing someone so close and beloved. Son, I forgive you for any pain you caused your mother, our family, and me in the way you were ripped from our lives. I recognize that you mourned as well. I selfishly acknowledge this book as part of my own healing process. As I wrote it, I was often in tears. I pray that my words may help a few others in their journeys to overcome their own grief and losses.

I also dedicate this book to Canyon's mother, my wife Cologne, whose hurt has been inconsolable at times, and to my children, Seantay, Kevin, Spencer, and Sierra, who loved Canyon dearly and looked up to him. You suffered so much. I am so proud of your growth and example. Thank you for your patience with me and all your sacrifices that afforded me the opportunity to write. May you find more peace and healing in these pages.

I also acknowledge Canyon's friends who supported him in life and supported us after his death. I hope this book will bring comfort to them.

I can't adequately thank all my family and friends and those who willingly helped me in the writing journey. Your hearts, advice, tears, and honest feedback inspired me and made the impossible possible.

I acknowledge all who encouraged me to write this book—especially that sweet older woman in the airport. I never got your name. You allowed me to help you in a moment of trial, and you gave me the encouragement I needed. Thank you.

—Sean M. Fleming

# INTRODUCTION

# DOUBTS ARE TRAITORS

*"Our doubts are traitors,
and make us lose the good
we oft might win,
by fearing to attempt."*

~ William Shakespeare

Ten years and a few months after the tragic and sudden death of my son, I've finally found the courage to publish this book. The resistance and obstacles I met on the way were real and varied. Excuses and fear were sometimes prevalent and seemed to creep up and wrangle my progress in insidious ways, convincing me of things that were not necessarily true. *I don't need to publish it.* I didn't need to, but in the journey of writing and letting others read it, I grew, others were helped, and lives were improved. Some might benefit from my experience, and what a shame if I wasn't willing to share.

We all have a message we get to deliver, some subtle, some profound, but who will ever know if we don't overcome the resistance that seeks to thwart the message of light we all have inside us.

Though I've suffered great loss, I've been privileged to be in a place where, because of my intimate knowledge of pain and the pain around me, I could offer perspective and needed light in others lives. I don't claim any great knowledge, as a matter of fact I'm just a guy telling a vulnerable story, offering it up in hope that it will find its way to those who may benefit from it.

We all suffer loss of some kind in this life, loved ones, friends, family members, pets, jobs, income, savings, homes, and the list goes on. What we choose to focus on, however, determines our progress, degree of success, and, ultimately, happiness in any journey upon which we embark—especially the challenging journey of life.

I have met husbands and wives, and brothers and sisters of individuals who have taken their own lives or passed on from tragedy. Some of these people never let go of the guilt, the pain, or the need for more answers. This failure to release the pain is as much a tragedy as their loved ones' deaths. In most cases, the person who died (accidentally or through suicide) wouldn't want his or her loved ones to suffer forever in constant prisons of self-doubt, guilt, or blame that could ruin their lives.

I had an enlightening experience one afternoon that turned out to be a perfect example of how tragedy can beget more tragedy if we don't consciously commit to recovering from our losses and allowing ourselves to heal.

I was driving from Palm Springs to the Los Angeles/Ontario Airport. I had planned to reach the airport with just enough time to check in and board my flight, but as

# Introduction

I was checking out of my hotel, things took a little longer than I had expected. I probably wouldn't be late, but I would be cutting it very close. As I drove, almost as though I sensed a hint of fate in the air, I made up my mind that whatever happened today would be exactly what needed to happen. I'd stay committed to making my flight and to doing everything I could to make it on time, including going a little over the legal speed limit. If I were supposed to make my flight, I would. If something else were intended to happen for me, that would manifest itself as well. I think this unusual perspective made me open to what happened next.

As I got to the rental company, nobody was outside to check in cars. You had to go into the office if you wanted a receipt, and that would take a long time. So I left the rental car with the keys in the ignition at the drop-off and ran to catch the shuttle bus. Amazingly, as I got to the curb, so did the bus. Just as I stepped through its door, the bus drove off as if it had showed up especially for me. Now, everything seemed to be pointing to me making my flight by lining up just right.

I got to the terminal, ran in and . . . they wouldn't give me a boarding pass. Now remember, I was at the Ontario Airport. It was exactly thirty minutes before my flight was to leave, late in the morning on a weekday, with very few people in the airport, yet the airline decided it was going to enforce the thirty-minute check-in rule that day, no exceptions. I could see that the security line was practically empty. I knew it wouldn't take me more than five minutes to get through security, and the gate my flight was leaving from was less than a two-minute walk from the security check point. I could have made it, easily.

I smiled at the clerk and told her that my watch showed a little different time than hers. I said I was sure she wouldn't mind helping me get home to my family because both of us knew I could board in the next ten minutes, which would be twenty minutes before the plane was scheduled to leave. I thought my request seemed reasonable, and with my big smile and a positive attitude, I was sure she would let me through.

"No," she said. "That won't be happening today. You can use the phone right over there to schedule a new flight." Are you kidding me? I didn't say it, but I sure thought it. Instead, I smiled, even thanked her for trying, and went to the phone she had indicated. Meanwhile, the nice people behind me also were denied the very same flight. I rescheduled to a flight more than three hours later, paid the fee to do so over the phone, and sat down to contemplate why I hadn't made the flight. However, because I'd made the decision earlier that *whatever happens will be just right*, I decided there must be something else I needed to be open to. With nothing more to do, I sat back and watched as the family members who had been behind me in line, now in tears, were denied their flight. I overheard them say they were headed to a funeral they would probably miss if they didn't catch this flight. They were denied boarding despite their best attempts at negotiation, including arguments, pleading, and even crying.

Because I had just gone through the same situation, I was aware of all the flight options they had, including hiring a taxi to take them to a different airport where they could catch another flight that would allow them still to make it in time for the funeral. I walked up to them to offer my

# Introduction

assistance. They were grateful for my advice about catching the flight out of the nearby airport. As the father made those arrangements, we spoke of their dear friend who had just died at a very young age in a car accident. They were traveling to be with his family at this time of loss. They reserved the flight I suggested and left in a hurry, grateful for my help.

While I had been speaking to this family, the elderly woman next to me had been reading a book. Apparently, she had overheard my entire conversation with these people. As I sat down, she turned to me and said, "That was really nice, what you did. You should be proud of yourself." She paused and continued, "But there is something else I'd like to talk to you about, if you don't mind."

I've learned you never turn down a conversation with a grandma.

As I had talked to this family about their young friend, and how his parents were not doing well, I had also mentioned that I had lost my own son. I had related how difficult it is to lose a child, and that I knew from my own experience that it's nice to have friends like them. I had mentioned how it was valuable and important that they be there to help where they could, at least if nothing else to let their friends know how much they were loved. My elderly neighbor said she was impressed with what I had said because she had been troubled with what to do about her own son and his family. She said she felt compelled to talk with me, and she hoped I would forgive the intrusion.

"Please go on," I replied. "Besides, I'm not going anywhere for a while."

As it turned out, she had been denied the very same flight, just before me. She was on her way to Washington State with a layover in Salt Lake City. She was going to Washington to spend time with her grandchildren. Her son and his wife had lost one of their young children, the oldest of three. Her son hadn't dealt with the loss very well and had, as she put it, "drowned his sorrows in a bottle." She was sad because his wife and young children didn't have their father and husband through what was a difficult time for them too. In fact, they had recently divorced, partly due to the aftermath of their child's death. "They were such a beautiful family," she said. "They had such opportunity." Her son had taken on himself a lot of the blame for his son's death and hadn't been able to forgive himself. He doubted his ability to be a father. He doubted his worth, and as a result, his other children didn't have a father because he couldn't be there for them. In a sense, they had lost a sibling and then lost their father to his grief, self-blame, and self-doubt. Most people would call his behavior selfish (and it is that in many ways), but it seemed to me that his selfishness was really a result of his doubts and fears. His mother was now sad and troubled, but somehow, talking to me gave her some hope and relief.

We talked for some time. I'm not sure what inspired her, but as she complimented me for sharing and thanked me for listening to her, she insisted I should write a book. I laughed. Then I thanked her and said I had given it some serious thought, but I didn't know whether I really wanted to tell the world what had happened to my family and me. I doubted my ability to write a book, especially a personal one,

## INTRODUCTION

and I was afraid of being judged. Yet, she was encouraging and said it would be a shame if one person who needed to hear something like what she'd heard from me didn't get that chance because I refused to share.

That word struck me kind of hard. Refused.

"What if that one person were someone close to you, someone you knew? What if your book only helped one person? It might still be worth it," she insisted.

Something inside me, a deep instinct or knowing, told me she was right. A swell of emotion almost spilled over. It would be worth it, even if it only helped one person. I felt my own doubts tormenting me, telling me I wasn't worthy of such a task. I wasn't good enough. I knew none of those fears haunting me were true. I needed to trust myself, trust that instinct, and not let my head talk my heart out of what I knew was true. "Don't doubt," she said. "Do it!"

Like her son—a father who'd lost his son and was struggling with the loss—what a tragedy it would be if I didn't let go of my own self-doubts. I pray that he and I . . . and you . . . and all of us who have suffered loss and know the grief that accompanies it . . . can erase our doubts, forgive ourselves, and embrace the life that awaits us.

*"For all sad words of tongue or pen,*
*the saddest are these "it might have been."*

~ John Greenleaf Whittier

# LOSS

# THE DRAGONFLY

*"To live in the hearts we leave behind,*

*is not to die."*

~ Thomas Campbell

In 2002, the summer after the loss of my son Canyon, my ten-year-old son Kevin and I stood knee deep in the water of the Henry's Fork River. The river babbled contentedly around us. In front of us, the sun was starting to set. The diminishing light cast a soft pink hue over the serene landscape and clouds. It was one of those rare, magical moments in life where all time seems to stand still.

The perfect silence was interrupted by an intense vibrating sound coming from the meadow behind us as an unusually large, golden dragonfly swooped down past my son's fishing rod. The dragonfly was about four inches long and quite a noisy spectacle. Its wings sputtered in the air as it spun and dodged around Kevin, as if inviting him to play. The dragonfly landed, soft as silk, on a stick that lay on the side of the water. It seemed to be taking a drink from its new perch.

Kevin was mesmerized by the show, and I could tell he felt like he should get a closer look at this amazing creature. He broke the stillness by slowly walking through the water, trying not to make too much noise or any sudden movements that might scare the dragonfly away.

I watched, transfixed, as Kevin slid his feet through the water. He was careful not to lift his wading boots too far up, so they wouldn't splash the water as it rushed around him.

The dragonfly seemed to be staring at Kevin, with its two strangely big eyes that seemed to make up its entire head. As Kevin continued to get closer, I knew the moment wouldn't last much longer. Kevin got within just a couple of feet and then bent down ever so slowly and stretched out his hand. What happened next seems strange in retrospect, but at the moment, it seemed completely natural—as if they already knew what would happen next. Kevin held out his hand and the dragonfly accepted his offer.

The thin-bodied insect sat perched in Kevin's hand as he held it close to his face, slowly angling his hand to study the entire iridescent creature. He held it up against the pink dusk as he examined it and said simply, "Hi."

I stood hypnotized by the beauty of this exchange and my heart swelled with some unexplainable sentiment that made it feel huge. I didn't talk. I just watched as Kevin reached his hand up high to the sky and the golden dragonfly fluttered its wings and made a graceful circle around him as if to say goodbye. Then it headed off toward the meadow in the direction from which it came. Kevin watched as it disappeared from sight. He looked over at me, unaware I'd been watching him from behind the entire time. He smiled at me as if to say, *Can you believe it?*

# The Dragonfly

I smiled my agreement. We quietly resumed our fishing as the sun continued to set on the horizon.

Soon it was dark, and we decided to head back to the car. As we walked along the bank, Kevin shared with me that the golden dragonfly had made him feel whole, as if they were able to communicate their approval of each other. He said the moment seemed magical and he wondered why the dragonfly had let him hold it.

I told Kevin that the dragonfly was probably coming to the end of its life, and since it had already filled the measure of its creation, it was willing to take a risk. Why not go meet the interesting boy on the side of the river? There was nothing more to fear. I wasn't sure if I even believed my own explanation, but it came from a sincere place.

Kevin asked me why people don't do that more with their lives. Why aren't people more willing to take chances in order to have moments of magic? Wouldn't it be better if we and the dragonfly all lived like that our whole lives?

It was a brilliant question, one I couldn't adequately answer, but I still made an attempt. I told Kevin that life requires a certain balance of responsibility and risk. There are certain things we must accomplish in life and some of those things override the excitement we might get from taking a chance. For instance, I told him that I had a responsibility to keep him safe and to raise him with opportunities to learn and experience life in an environment that challenged but also nurtured him as he grew, until he could make his own decisions. If I put him in situations that risked his life or his physical or emotional health, I would be irresponsible. Although we might have a lot of fun, it would not be right.

In a dragonfly's life, there is an order to things. It might not fully understand that order, but the dragonfly knows instinctively to comply with it. After the dragonfly emerges from the water, it is compelled to mate so eggs can be laid and there can be more dragonflies. This impulse is so strongly built into the dragonfly that it must fulfill this natural law. Once the dragonfly completes it, there is opportunity to explore and enjoy on a different level. Then, the dragonfly can take more risk.

Again, I wasn't sure whether I believed what I had just told Kevin, but it seemed to make sense. It was the best explanation I could come up with. I could tell he was still thinking and had other questions. Then he said quietly, "I felt like it was trying to tell me something, something that I wanted and needed to know."

I didn't question Kevin about what that might be. I knew he'd tell me when he was ready, if it were something he wanted to share. I did, however, ask Kevin whether he had ever heard the story of the water bugs crawling up the lily pad. He said he hadn't. The experience with the dragonfly reminded me this story I'd heard as a child, so I shared it with him.

---

There were three little water bugs who lived and played under the water's surface, knowing nothing other than their world. They played constantly, and every once in a while watched another water bug crawl up and out of the water and onto the lily pad. Each time this happened, they noticed the water bug seemed to be different just before he crawled out, and he never came back. This event became quite a curiosity

# The Dragonfly

among the water bugs, and they grew concerned that the water bugs that left knew something they didn't know. Still, they continued to play.

One day as they watched another water bug crawl out and not return, they decided to make a pact. It was becoming apparent that one day they might have to do the same thing because these water bugs seemed to need to crawl out of the water. The water bugs promised each other that when one of them finally went up the lily pad stem, out of the water, and discovered what was up there beyond the water, that one would come back and tell the others what all the fuss was about. They all agreed and resumed their playing and eating.

One day, one of the three water bugs crawled right up that lily pad stem and out of the water. The two left behind were shocked and couldn't even play as they did every day. Instead, they sat there, motionless, waiting for him to come back. But he didn't come back!

Meanwhile, up on the lily pad, the first little water bug had stopped breathing water and was now breathing air. Breathing air felt good, and he felt considerably different. His wings were growing and he felt strange as he broke out of his shell and climbed out as a beautiful golden dragonfly. Other dragonflies were flying around and bouncing against the water trying to talk to their friends below the surface. He remembered the deal he had made with his buddies. He couldn't get back into the water, though, because he could no longer breathe water. The golden dragonfly stretched his wings. They felt amazing! He watched as the other dragonflies flew around the pond with the ease of angels. The dragonfly vibrated his wings and then was, to his amazement, in flight—as naturally as if he had always known how to fly. He flew around the pond as happy and excited as he had ever been.

This new place was magnificent, and he wondered how he had never known about it before. He thought of his friends again and swooped down, determined to keep his promise, but as he bounced across the surface of the water, he couldn't get back in. His friends would just have to find out for themselves when it was their time.

Below the surface, the two water bug buddies were quite anxious. After all, their friend had made a promise and water bug promises are law. Surely he would come back down, but he never did. All of a sudden, the second water bug said, "That's it! I've got to see what is going on up there!" But he wasn't ready, and when he went out, he couldn't breathe and quickly had to return to the water. He also couldn't see, so when he came back down to the third water bug, he knew no more than he had before he left. The water bugs felt betrayed and playing wasn't quite as much fun as it had once been. Instead, they ate more and more.

Then one day they felt different. They knew it was their day to go to the surface. They did, easily, and as they emerged, their friend, the first water bug, now a majestic golden dragonfly, landed right next to them.

They looked at him in amazement. They recognized their friend, though they could hardly believe how brilliant and golden he was. He told them he had been waiting for them, and it had been very hard to wait. He had tried to get back into the water, but he couldn't. He asked them to forgive him for not coming back, which of course they did. He told his friends that shortly they would be able to join him up in the air where there were marvelous things to see.

# The Dragonfly

Just as their friend had promised, the water bugs went through their magical transformations and emerged again as two majestic golden dragonflies. The three exquisite dragonflies flew off together, dancing and darting happily across the pond in the soft, pink light of the setting sun.

---

Kevin looked at me and smiled as if he had just discovered something important. "That's just like Canyon," he said knowingly. "He went to a new place, a place we can't go to yet. If he could, he would probably come back and tell us all about it. It's probably much nicer than here, and he is amazed at the freedom he has. He can probably even fly around with ease. We're just like the second and third water bugs that want to know more but have to wait. We should be happy for him and play more 'til it's our time to go up and out of the water. He'd want to know we had fun and didn't worry about him."

"Kevin, you're a very wise little water bug and I couldn't agree more," I said, unable to get the lump out of my throat as we walked along the trail and back to our car. If the sun hadn't already dipped below the horizon, it would have been easy for him to see the tears running down my face.

# LOST CANYON

*"We find in life exactly what we put into it."*

~Ralph Waldo Emerson

AT DIFFERENT POINTS IN OUR LIVES, we have experiences we'll never forget. At the time, we don't always realize how memorable the moment will be. Yet for one reason or another, the memory never leaves us. Even if we're not exactly sure why, the impression is too deep ever to forget. I had one of those experiences as a boy when my father took my family to a very special place near our home in Eagle, Idaho. I call it Lost Canyon.

It was early summer, and I was six years old. I had just finished first grade, and I was so ready for a summer adventure. Our old white Volvo sedan, with its burgundy wine-colored vinyl seats and black, perpetually dusty dashboard, moved us along toward our destination. As we drove in the direction of the foothills north of Eagle, the small town in Idaho where we'd recently moved, we could tell this day was going to be special.

My father just had that look in his eyes that said he was up to something. We were full of childlike anticipation.

My siblings and I loved spending time with our parents on these excursions. Mom and Dad always had a way of making them exciting and memorable. As we drove through the countryside, I had no idea what was in store or what deep impact it would later have in my life.

We four kids—my two brothers, my sister, and me—were crammed in the back of our old, hot car that was filled with the unmistakable stale scent of dust and hot vinyl. There was no air conditioner; only the open side wing windows provided circulation. Since there were four of us, two kids were always in the middle, sharing one seat belt, while the two kids on the ends each had his or her own seat belt, and, of course a window. An outside seat was a coveted place worth fighting for, and we often did, until Mom or Dad intervened to impose their form of justice, called "taking turns."

The engine in our little car strained as it worked to pull us up the hill. I could almost feel its tension and effort as I sat in the backseat. My body was stretched as tall as I could make it, so I could see out the windows. I hadn't been lucky enough to get a window seat that day, but I was still determined to enjoy whatever view I could get. My parents were sticklers for seat belts, before seat belts were even popular, so my right leg was bent between my rear end and the seat. I got more lift that way, so I could see out better. If my parents had caught me sitting on my foot and inching up, they would have told me to sit on the seat, not my foot. My leg and foot were going to sleep fast from lack of blood, but I didn't care. I didn't want to miss a moment from fear I might lose out on something important. My anticipation grew as I strained to see the dirt road my father was driving up. It was narrow and our car tires had to straddle a deep rut.

I admired my father's courage. As usual, what he was doing seemed amazing. As he balanced the car over the deep ruts that other vehicles had carved into the muddy road before us, he completely focused on his task. It was rough terrain and we all felt a bit anxious and excited, yet he seemed to be enjoying himself, which made the adventure especially fun for the rest of us.

As we broke over the top of the hill, I think we were all holding our breaths. Even the engine of the car sounded relieved as it seemed to take in a deep breath of air as we crested the hill. Finally, we were out of the shade and into the sunlight as we came out of the ravine.

The grass seemed to be dancing and waving in the breeze, welcoming us. Its new blades glistened in the sunlight. They would soon be amber-colored and dry, but now, in the spring, they were green and lush with little purple flowers mixed in, giving the hillsides a purple hue.

As the nose of the car dipped down, we were able to see over the front dashboard, and what we saw caused us to gasp in surprise. A huge crack in the earth before us looked like God had swung a mighty sword and split the earth. It was unexpected and didn't seem real. We were speechless for a brief moment and then erupted into shrill cries of childhood delight, amazement, and excitement.

My father pulled up near the canyon's edge, fearlessly driving up to the ravine, embracing adventure. Looking back on the experience, I recognize how cautious he actually was with his rambunctious little herd. He gave instructions for us to stay in the car as it came to a stop and asked us to stay close to him when we got out of the car. We followed his orders, even though our legs wanted to run and explore. I wouldn't have gotten far, however, because as I got out of the car I realized my right leg was asleep from sitting on it. It felt like I was wearing a thick cast, and my leg tingled with sharp prickly sensations all over. I almost fell over as I got out of the car.

Dad carefully led his little brood to the edge and let us perch on a large rock a short distance from the edge of the canyon wall. From there, we could see 270 degrees of the canyon's beauty as it swept around us. The deep and rocky wonderland was mysteriously carved into the foothills. It seemed out of place, yet completely where it belonged. We could see a small creek at the bottom of the canyon and hear it babbling. It seemed to be calling to us with a cool, soothing whisper.

The light breeze caressed our faces and blew our hair. The air was dry and the sagebrush smell in the air was so fragrant that it tickled my nose. Allergies were a problem for me when I was young, so sure enough, the sneezing fits started right up, but just like my sleepy leg, I wouldn't let them distract me. Red eyes and a runny nose were a minor price to pay to see such a splendid and amazing sight.

While other kids were taking summer vacation trips with their parents to the Grand Canyon, my parents did their best to make us feel special by taking us on smaller trips. They were struggling to make ends meet, but I didn't know it at the time. I was being introduced to what I thought was a Grand Canyon of its own. Even if I had known our canyon was a speck compared to the Grand Canyon, it would have made no difference to me. This canyon was more spectacular than anything I had ever seen.

I looked down at my pants and noticed their color matched one of the rocks of the canyon wall. My rust-colored denim jeans had been handed down from someone else we knew—just about everything we wore was handed down. Holes in both knees of my pants had been lovingly patched up by my mother. I was glad there wasn't a patch on this big hole in the earth. I seriously wanted to climb down inside and explore this new wonderland.

Like most little boys, I had an affinity for rocks, and this mysterious rocky retreat was just begging to be explored. The rocks were unlike anything I had ever seen. The colors were so vivid they almost looked artificial. They melted together in patterns and swirls, as if made of saltwater taffy, where the creator had not quite finished mixing up the batch. The swirling reds, whites, and ambers mixed into shimmering dark burgundies, rusts, and browns. They reminded me of candy. *Oh, if only I could just reach out and take a big bite,* I thought. *I wonder how it would taste.*

There were long sharp rock segments that looked like they had peeled off the canyon wall and then reattached to the side. They defied gravity as they clung to the side of the cliffs. A large hawk flew above us in the air on the canyon's other side. As it drew my attention upward, I heard it cry out, as if giving me my own personal greeting.

I watched as the hawk hovered effortlessly in the same spot above us, allowing invisible wind currents to hold him. His wings moved ever so slightly, using the breeze to his advantage as he paused over the canyon and surveyed his domain. The same breeze that held the hawk effortlessly above caressed my face and lightly ruffled my hair. The breeze felt good, and the comforting warmth it had gathered from the sun-baked rocks was hypnotic.

My father interrupted my mouth-wide-open gawking by asking us to follow him. We hiked down a small hill that led away from the edge, then around to the top end of the canyon. New emerald grasses were just coming up and felt like a lush green carpet under our feet. Scattered patches of yellow and purple flowers, with a splash of bright red and orange, adorned our path.

As the afternoon sun shone down over the edge of the canyon wall, we soon found ourselves alongside a creek that led to the canyon's mouth. I could hardly walk straight because I was looking up and all around, not watching where I stepped. I stumbled several times and almost fell into the creek more than once. This was heaven, as I knew it. I was in paradise. Bright patches of lichen, which looked as though someone had splashed thin layers of orange and yellow mustard mixed with green relish all over the rocks above us, covered the canyon walls.

We scrambled around boulders and in and out of the water. We found rock treasures to take home and threw others we found in the water, making big splashes, and cheered loudly at our feats of strength. The sounds we made echoed at times, encouraging us to get louder and louder in hopes of hearing our voices thrown back to us again. I found a shady spot against the canyon wall next to the creek. Green moss was on the shaded ground where it felt cool to the touch. It felt good in contrast to the increasing heat of the day. I sat down on a mossy patch, lay back, and stretched my arms to cool my neck and body.

Just as I felt like its cooling touch had restored some strength to my overheated body, I heard Dad call out that it was time to go. We'd been there for a couple of hours, but it seemed like only a few minutes. In answer to my protest, he assured me we would return soon.

As we drove home that day, my mind played back memories of that fantastically special place. My father had introduced it to us in such a way that we felt as if we were the only ones who even knew it existed. It seemed hidden and secret.

As I grew older, Lost Canyon became a special place, sort of a spiritual spot that I could visit when I wanted to think and ponder my life's situations. I'd go there sometimes when I needed a break or just wanted to be alone. I took others out to the canyon, hoping it would be as cool and special to them as it was to me. My buddies and I even camped there often. We rappelled, climbed the rock walls, caught rattlesnakes, and found more rock treasures. We played, we gained experience, and we grew. It was an oasis from the mundane routines of daily living. Little did I know at the time it would also turn out to be an oasis from the unthinkable heartbreak life would later bring me.

# THE BEGINNING

The music played loudly as I walked into the dance. The spot seemed to vibrate and bounce with energy. I was twenty-one years old, and it seemed that everything was there just for me. It was an amazing time in life, which rolled from one exciting activity to another, with lots of new people. That night, a few of my friends and I had decided to go to a dance in Davis, California to meet girls. We had driven from Sacramento, where I lived.

When I walked into the dance, I scanned the room. I saw many attractive young women. Fearless and frightened at the same time, I approached one and asked her to dance. I would dance with several different girls that night, blissfully unaware that my life was about to change forever.

I'd just finished a dance when my friend Glen grabbed me by the arm and said, "Sean, I want to introduce you to someone."

When I turned around, standing in front of me was the

woman of my dreams, with long, dark, wavy hair and tan skin. Her dark eyes drew me in like a gravity vortex from a science fiction movie. They were remarkably deep and seemingly endless. Her smile made my knees weak and my tongue froze in my throat. I barely got out the words, "Hi, my name's Sean."

"I'm Cologne," she said with a smile; her eyes drilled into mine as time stood still. I felt like an idiot, but I didn't even care.

And that was it. All my bravado was gone. I was left to wonder what to do next. I had nothing else. I'd been taught that one of the best ways to receive more inspiration is to act on the inspiration you've already received. Well, I was inspired, and I wanted to ask her to dance more than anything, but her brown eyes had me under a spell. I couldn't act. She never stopped smiling. Fortunately, Glen had my back and helped me with the next step. He put his hand on my shoulder and pushed Cologne and me toward the dance floor.

"Why don't you two go dance?" he said.

It was more of an order than a question. We talked and danced our way through a couple of songs. I didn't want to stop, but I reluctantly said goodbye after thanking her for dancing with me. As I walked away, I glanced back and caught her still watching me. She smiled at me and I smiled back. A few minutes went by as we mingled with others around the room until we were standing in front of each other again. In unison, we asked, "Do you want to dance?"

We didn't dance with anyone else the rest of the evening. We spent most of the time on the dance floor. I didn't know what was going on inside me, but I decided to surrender to it.

That night was incredible. As we said goodbye to each other again, she invited me to a party the next evening. She

# The Beginning

said she wanted to see me again and wanted to introduce me to some friends in the singing group to which she belonged. I knew that was a good sign, her wanting to introduce me to her friends. The group was going to perform at the World's Fair in Brisbane, Australia in June. *She sings, too? I thought. What other magical things don't I know about her?*

The next day seemed to drag on forever. I couldn't wait to see the brown-eyed girl again. When I showed up at the party, we saw each other from across the room. I still remember vividly the charge that surged through my body when I saw her. When she smiled, I knew she was happy to see me too. We went directly outside and talked for hours. No one else mattered.

The night we met, one of my friends told me I needed to be careful because Cologne had a two-year-old son. His remarks didn't faze me at all. I couldn't even imagine not being with Cologne. I ached to know more about her. She made me feel weak and invincible at the same time. She had a mystery about her that I needed to solve, and my soul was thirsting for answers.

On the second evening, I found out she'd been trying to break up with her boyfriend, but he wasn't letting her go very easily. It was clear to me that another guy at the party obviously liked her too. I'd never had such competition for a girl before, but I knew she was worth it.

My mother and sister were in the kitchen when I walked in the next day. I made small talk, but after a few minutes, I found myself talking alone. They were staring at me with big eyes and huge smiles. I looked at them with a puzzled look and wondered, *What are you two up to?* They turned to each other, nodded knowingly, and reported the obvious in unison, "You're in love." Indeed, they had me pegged. I was in love.

Later that night, I knocked on her door and waited. The porch light was off and it was dark outside. Cologne opened the door, quietly slid out as if in secret, and carefully closed the door behind her. We stood face to face on the front porch in the dark. I wanted to kiss her. She held her hands behind her back since she still had hold of the doorknob. "There's someone I want you to meet," she said.

"Okay," I said, somewhat anxiously.

She turned around, opened the door, and asked me to follow her. We went into the house and up the stairs. When she got to the top of the stairs, she turned and opened a bedroom door. I followed right behind, feeling a little uncertain.

"Meet my son, Canyon," she said. There before me on the bed sat the cutest little boy I'd ever seen. He was wearing a pair of blue and red shorts, and no shirt. His skin was tan, his hair was straight and sandy brown, and he had the same eyes that had placed me into a hypnotic spell just nights before. He looked just like her. I was excited and confused, fearless and unsure at the same time. So many questions.

She smiled at me. I didn't ask any questions. She assumed I already knew she had a child, which I guess I did. She made no apologies. She was graceful and confident, and Canyon was obviously a very happy child.

"Hello, Canyon. How old are you?" I asked.

He quickly pointed at me with two fingers and smiled a big smile. As I smiled back, he stood up on the bed and gave me a big hug. I'd already fallen in love with Cologne, but at that moment, I fell in love with both of them.

# The Beginning

It didn't take long for me to ask Cologne to marry me. Our engagement lasted about nine months before we got married in July 1988, after she returned from performing at the World's Fair in June.

A commitment to Cologne came with a commitment to Canyon, so I was thrown head first into parenting. I had an instant family. It was a lot of pressure, but everything just seemed right. I questioned my ability to handle it all a few times, but those worries passed quickly. Looking back on it, I wonder whether I was just young and naïve, or really that brave. Either way, I had a fabulous wife with an angelic son. He called me Sean for the first year, and then started calling me Daddy on his own.

I adopted Canyon not long after our marriage, and as far as he and I were concerned, he was my son. He'd had contact with his biological father only once when he was just a baby. That man cared enough for Canyon to give me permission to adopt him when I asked. Our lives were blessed, the three of us . . . all of us growing up together. We seemed to have the world by the tail, a long and wagging tail. We hung on tight, and did our best to act like we knew what we were doing.

# A "PERFECT" FAMILY

THE SECOND SEPTEMBER OF OUR MARRIAGE, Cologne gave birth to Seantay, a little ball of hair with more energy and determination than all three of us combined. I was instantly smitten with her, and she has kept me in a trance ever since. She was born with a cleft pallet, which made the first few months before she had reconstructive surgery very difficult. Often exhausted, Cologne spent hours trying to feed Seantay. She had left her singing group to be a mother and take care of her family, as well as giving up other personal ambitions and desires. Being a stay-at-home mother was a lot of work, but it was how we wanted to raise our children, and although it was a big sacrifice on her part, it was extremely valuable to our little family.

With Cologne's efforts, Seantay grew stronger and more determined. Even though the first few months of her life before reconstructive surgery were difficult, she gained a winning personality. Canyon was with her one hundred percent of the time, always helping with his new little sister.

Kevin, our third child, came into our lives in December 1991. He was an easy child to care for, and he was extremely playful from the start. He was instantly a great blessing to our family and had a fantastic disposition. From the time he was very young, he has had an attitude that anything is possible. Our three children found much to do together. Canyon usually initiated the activity, Seantay turned it into a bit of mischief, and Kevin was the one to carry it out and make everyone laugh in the process with his happy-go-lucky nature. The three kids were inseparable, and Canyon was a caring big brother to them.

In January 1996, during one of the worst winter storms Salt Lake City had seen in the last century, Spencer, our third son, was born; his birth metaphorically ushered a new storm into our lives, the most challenging storm yet. We couldn't have been prepared for what we'd need to know and do in order to care for him.

Spencer was born completely deaf, with multiple birth defects, and severe autism. He spent most of the first year of his new life at Primary Children's Hospital. There were times when we didn't know whether he would make it through the night. Nine of his multiple surgeries took place that first year. We seemed to live at the hospital. It was extremely hard on us at times, especially for Cologne, who was dealing with Spencer's primary care and the additional considerations his unique condition required.

We had already experienced many challenges, but instantly, we became acquainted with much greater challenges when this little guy entered our lives.

## A "Perfect" Family

Spencer has been a blessing. He helps us recognize and appreciate many things, especially what it means to be well and healthy. He is a little piece of heaven in our home with his pure innocence.

For the next five years, Spencer was in and out of the hospital for various surgeries and sicknesses. Cologne was an extremely busy mother, caring for four children, one of whom required constant care. She hardly got a break. I did what I could to help, most of which came too little or too late.

We just kept putting one foot in front of the other. We experienced some beautiful moments that seemed quite meaningful, as well as those that were awkward and difficult. At times, we didn't know whether we would survive. Sometimes people said things such as, "Wow, I sure admire you guys for handling life with a handicapped child as well as you do," or, "I don't know how you do it." We didn't either. We did it because we didn't know any differently. We didn't have a choice. We had each other, and we relied on each other. It wasn't always pretty, it certainly wasn't graceful, but our simple inexperienced understanding of life allowed us to keep moving forward, no matter what happened.

Several years after having Spencer, my career was really advancing and I was becoming one of the more recognized commercial real estate agents in the area. After years of financial trials and children needing medical care, it was a welcome blessing. Cologne was starting to enjoy a small reprieve from the daily worries of caring for Spencer, and we had pretty much decided we were finished having children. Quietly, I wanted more children, but caring for Spencer had taken a lot out of Cologne. She admitted she wasn't sure about having another child with the trials we'd had with both Spencer and Seantay. Basically, Cologne was done and asked me to make sure of it. She wanted no risk of having another child, and who could blame her? I remember being in my office with the urologist's phone number on my desk. I'd been glancing at it for a few weeks, and I wondered whether I should just commit and go for it. I'm not sure whether I was being a chicken about the procedure or I just didn't feel right about it. Either way, I knew Cologne's opinion.

The receptionist interrupted my thoughts to tell me that my wife was on line two. I picked up the phone and gave my usual greeting, "Hey, Babe."

I was leaning back in the chair with my knees pushed up against the desk propping me back. I felt pretty cavalier about what I'd accomplished for the day.

"Are you sitting down?" she asked.

"Yes, I am," I replied, expecting some exciting news.

"I'm pregnant," she said in a low, deep voice that had a tone that sounded like... *you evil man.*

She threw the words at me like a fastball pitcher who knows the catcher isn't ready. The line went silent. I didn't respond and she didn't say a thing. I felt my face go pale as the blood drained out of it, and I almost fell back onto the floor. In this dazed state, I somehow had the presence of mind to know I needed to be happy or at least console her, but being happy came with the fear of how she might take my happiness, a fear that she wouldn't be happy at all but would resent me for any celebration.

Cologne enjoyed being a mother, but her pregnancies had been difficult, and raising a disabled son had created in her a swell of emotions I didn't adequately know how to help with. She was home with the kids all day, and it was difficult for her to get a break. I did what I could to help, but what I thought would help usually didn't.

We loved each other, but at times, we were pretty sure we didn't know why, and we wondered whether we'd made a mistake in getting married. At this time, we seemed to be in a phase where we were working hard on our marriage and trying to find ways for Cologne to get a break. Certainly not new ways to encumber her.

Apparently, God had other plans.

"We're going to be okay," I said tentatively. "There must be a reason for this because we've been pretty careful."

I immediately chastised myself. *What an idiot you are*, I thought. *Don't you have anything better than that?* I didn't know what I was most worried about, and at the same time, I inherently knew I should be happy. I told her I loved her, I'd be there for her, and we were being blessed. I told her this pregnancy would be different because she deserved to have a good pregnancy. She calmly reminded me that we had no insurance. I assured her that the financial part would be all right, too. *Now I just have to convince myself*, I thought, feeling queasy.

We said goodbye after she assured me she was fine and was actually more worried about me. Funny, I was worried about her, and she was worried about me. My concern didn't end there, however.

I got up and walked out of the office. I took the elevator to the first floor, and for nearly two hours, I walked around downtown in a cloudy daze, hoping and praying that my wife would be okay emotionally, and that things would work out. I was worrying about something I had no ability to control, which wasn't like me, but I was excited at the same time. I was a wreck.

Sierra was born in May 2001. She is perfect in every way and brought an inspiring season of spring into our lives, literally and figuratively. Cologne's pregnancy went well, and we were blessed with a sweet little angel. The whole family was old enough to help with Sierra, and she was passed back and forth from Mom to Canyon to Seantay to Kevin and then to me. She was completely spoiled with attention and well cared for. She brightened our days and comforted our nights more than we could have ever imagined. God must have known how much we were going to need this little angel in our lives.

We were a loving, happy family of seven. We felt like we'd paid our dues in trials. We'd grown tremendously through our adversity. We knew more was in store in terms of growth and learning, but we felt good about the future. Surely, we would get a break from hardships. Surely, it was time for some smooth sailing. I guess we were still innocent in our thinking at that point. We still thought a life of comparative peace was a possibility.

What I've finally come to terms with is that while life can be frequently brilliant and joyful, the sea doesn't stay perfectly calm for long, and eventually other storms will hit, some more devastating than others.

# PRELUDE TO BROKEN HEARTS

December 8, 2001 was an unusually warm day for December. It was a pleasant day, one of those days where it seems that nothing can go wrong. That morning it felt like, for some reason, the heavens seemed to favor us, and everything easily fell into place. Life seemed bright. I had a houseful of happy children. I was in the role of the fearless leader to my brood of five, as my father had once been to me. We had no indication it would be a day that would change our future forever and be a turning point in the lives of many others.

We had moved into our new home the first week of April. The home itself wasn't new, but it was new to us. Sierra was born just weeks after we moved in. It had all worked out perfectly. Our spring had been busy, but a satisfying kind of busy.

We spent the summer fitting into our new house and making it a home. Finally, in December, life was settling down a bit and we felt good. We had a gorgeous new home. Everyone was healthy and well, except for five-year-old Spencer, but at least he was out of the hospital and over the life-threatening trials of his earlier years. Cologne had recovered well from giving birth to Sierra, who was just a little dream. The kids loved our new neighborhood, had made good friends, and fit in extremely well. Our financial health was better than it had ever been, and I was very pleased with my career and boldly considering starting my own land development company.

It promised to be a joyful holiday season. Cologne had wanted an "amazing" Christmas tree that year, one that was taller and fit better in our new home. She had gotten her wish, and we had all helped put it up right after Thanksgiving, as part of our yearly tradition. The tree was covered with detailed handmade wooden ornaments Cologne had made herself.

As in years past, Spencer's gift of new animals for his mobile was wrapped and under the tree with a few others. He would routinely twirl and flip his little toys all day long, while acting oblivious to anything else going on around him. It originally started when he discovered the little animals on his mobile over his crib. As soon as he was able to get up and grab one, he would never let go. They have been his companions ever since. In fact, those little animals were the only toy he would play with. They were his gift every birthday and Christmas.

That year, Kevin was excited about Christmas and his birthday on the 22nd. He had become our peacemaker child. His contagious smile radiated a confidence and passion for living that spilled out onto everyone he saw. His sandy brown hair was straight and thick. His brown eyes were warm enough to melt whatever they were looking at, and he had a way about him that was innocent and sweet. Kevin was always interested in other people. He was very helpful and obedient. He was only nine years old that holiday season, but that very night he and his sister would be hurled into a brutal reality that would force them to grow up faster than any child should ever have to.

Seantay was now twelve. She was a huge help and always willing to jump in and give assistance with whatever she could. She had long brown hair and the same hazel brown eyes all my children were blessed with from their mother. The only difference was that Seantay's eyes have a little splash of green you can see when the light is just right. They are stunning and reflect how she is the life of the party. She was mischievous at times, always hatching one plan or another, but she had a heart of gold. She always looked out for her siblings. She and Kevin were great friends and played well together. She would hatch a rascally plan and Kevin always seemed to get sucked into helping her carry it out. She looked up to Canyon. She was certain he could do no wrong in this world. She idolized him and was his biggest fan and supporter.

Canyon, the oldest of our children, was now sixteen. He was a marvelous boy. He did what he was asked, without complaint for the most part, and always seemed to go the extra mile. He loved everyone, and his infectious smile made him an instant friend. He had an easy time communicating with others and was easy to be around. He had changed a lot the last few years. Like many boys, he still loved video games and was extremely good at them. Hockey had become his sport of choice, and he was on the high school team. When it came to intellectual endeavors, he was immediately "all in," still with no reservations, and he had been that way from the time he was very young. Puzzles, games, and riddles were like candy to him. He consumed them quickly and wanted more. He had just ordered an adapter for his TI 86 calculator and couldn't wait for it to arrive. He'd recently started dating, which was new for us since he'd been more into video games than girls. Girls had noticed him for a while, but he'd been completely oblivious to them until recently. He'd always been a bit of a "nerd," a fact he proudly admitted, and though not considered popular, he was well liked by his peers.

That night, Cologne and I went out for dinner and a movie together. Canyon held his baby sister Sierra in his arms while Cologne and I said goodbye and left the kids in his care. He had been baby-sitting since he was eleven years old, and since he was very responsible and kind with children, we were grateful that he would watch his siblings so we could get out occasionally.

I hugged the two of them goodbye, and Canyon held Sierra's little hand up to make it look like she was waving to us as he squeaked out a tiny high-pitched "goodbye," as if Sierra were the one saying it. His smile was contagious. It made me smile back. Earlier in the day, he had gotten in trouble for not completing some things his mother and I had asked him to do. We were disappointed and had sternly lectured him. He had apologized, and we thought everything felt better as we exchanged hugs.

Next we hugged Seantay and Kevin, and I rubbed Spencer's head affectionately after giving him a kiss on the cheek. He didn't seem to care much that we're leaving. He was in what I refer to as "Spencer Land" as he sat on the floor and twirled his little mobile toys, seemingly oblivious to the world around him.

As Cologne and I got into the car and drove off, I thought about how grateful I was for my children and how good they were. I thought how nice it was that Canyon was responsible enough to watch the kids. I felt how blessed we all were and wondered what our future would hold.

As we drove to the restaurant, I looked over at Cologne. She looked stunning. She smiled back at me, which made me happy. I loved her smile. Little did I know it would be the last time I'd see that smile for a very long time.

# THE PHONE CALL

My cell phone rings. It's the kids. They seldom ever call when Cologne and I are out because Canyon does such a good job watching them. Cologne and I have been enjoying a good conversation about our future, and the server has just placed dinner in front of us. I've just taken a bite of my steak when the cell phone rings.

When I answer, Seantay and Kevin are screaming through the phone. Not just the usual kind of kids screaming, but sending out horrified, make-the-hairs-on-the-back-of-your-neck-stand-up screaming. I can't understand what they are saying. It sounds like they are fighting with each other, and I feel a bit annoyed that they are interrupting the nice evening I'm enjoying with their mother.

Somehow, among all the screams and chaos, I hear Seantay, breathless and scared, say at the top of her lungs, as if they are the last words she'll ever be able to say, "Canyon blew his head off with a gun, Daddy! His head is on your bed . . . his head is on your bed!"

The only thing I understand from Kevin, who is screaming in unison with Seantay, is, "There's blood everywhere, Daddy. Canyon shot his head off and I think I stepped in his brains."

I used to have a dream where I needed to shout out a warning but nothing would come out of my mouth. In the dream, my voice was bound and I couldn't speak. Despite my best efforts, I couldn't say what I needed to say. I would wake up from these dreams, exhausted and sweaty, frustrated that I couldn't speak when I needed to. I couldn't sound the warning.

This moment feels hauntingly like that dream. The energy and power of their desperate plea, the words I hear my two innocent and precious children say on the phone that evening will forever be stuck inside me. Only I heard those words, no one else, and few will ever know what it sounds like to hear those words coming from such innocent mouths. It will haunt me forever.

Cologne's smile is now gone, replaced by a look of fear. She doesn't know what the children have said, but she knows from the expression on my face that something is dreadfully wrong. I hang up the phone. My hand shuts it without consciously meaning to. To this day, I don't understand why I hung up the phone. I was confused and my mind was in shock from hearing those horrible words and worrying what to do or how to help my children. I guess my immediate reaction to hearing such unbelievable things

# The Phone Call

was simply to disconnect, and that was, literally, what I did without knowing it.

I quickly stand up from the table, hand Cologne my wallet, and abruptly say, "Pay for dinner; I need to call the kids back." Our table isn't far from the front lobby of the restaurant, so I run to where I can hear and call my children back to find out what is going on, to tell them what to do, and let them know I am coming, but . . . no answer! I try a couple of times. I don't know what to do. It's a bad dream. No way would my children do this to play a joke on me. They are much too thoughtful to say or do something this horrible. It has to be real. But on the other hand, it can't be true. There is no possible way that what I heard could be true. Yet, I can't take any chances. I call 911. I tell the dispatcher there's a problem at my home with my children and I need them to get there right away. I tell them that my son may have shot himself. I give them my address and hang up.

I hurry back to the table where Cologne is trying to take care of our bill with the waitress. They both look frazzled. Without even realizing it, I hand my entire wallet to the confused waitress, and we leave. Cologne has asked me a few times what's wrong, but I don't answer. I don't know how to answer. What can I say? I still hope it is all a bad dream and everything will be okay at home. How do I wake up from this dream? Cologne doesn't ask me again after we leave the restaurant, but she keeps praying out loud, asking God to protect our children.

The drive home seems endless. I keep trying to call home, but there is no answer. All the way home I feel like I am suffocating. I am short of breath and unable to find any air to breathe. Where are my children and why won't anyone answer the phone?

The drive is insufferably long. I cut every corner I can. I try to be calm for Cologne, but there's no doubt that something is very wrong at our home. Cologne doesn't cry, but she is engulfed in smothering fear. I wait until we turn into our subdivision, and then I tell her that Seantay and Kevin told me Canyon had shot himself. She gasps in horror as we turn the corner. We see the glow of red flashing lights in our cul-de-sac three streets up to the left. As I race to our street, police and fire trucks have it blocked. I swerve right and drive up over the curb and onto the grass of our neighbor's lawn. I slam the car into park and jump out, already running for the house.

Cologne jumps out of the car as well, but, screaming, she sinks to the ground. Her legs won't work. She can't follow. I run past friends standing on the sidewalk in front of the house. As I run by, they ask what they can do. Ignoring them, I keep running. I look back for Cologne and see that a few women have run to assist her. I keep running.

There is an ambulance in front of the house. Police are everywhere, and as I cross my lawn, one of them grabs me. Others come to help him hold me back. They don't know who I am. My home is a crime scene. I feel the bulletproof vests under their shirts as I press against them while they force me to hold still.

One of them yells into my face forcibly to find out who I am. My submission gives way to tears. "I'm his father."

They let me go. The one standing in front of me, who is obviously in charge, puts his hand on my chest. He looks

# The Phone Call

into my eyes. I can read his eyes like a book. I don't know whether he has children, but with all of the compassion of a father he says, "Sir, I can't stop you from going into your own home, but please take my advice. You can't do anything, and nothing good can come from you going inside right now. Please, take my word for it. Don't go in yet."

With that, it's final. There is no hope for me to do anything. It is over. I start to choke for air as I fall to the ground and begin to soak the lawn with tears that flow like they have never done before in my life. I feel as though my heart might stop. My chest seizes up with a kind of foreign pain I've never before experienced. The officer kneels beside me and puts his hand on my back. I don't know this man, but I feel his love and compassion. I see the image of Canyon's face in my mind. It's the image of him holding Sierra the last time I saw him, his smile infectiously huge. I gasp for air, trying to breathe, trying to stay alive. I think I might suffocate.

Moments later, I realize I haven't seen my other children. Where are Sierra, Spencer, Seantay, and Kevin? Are they safe? I jump up. A surge of adrenaline gives me the strength of ten men. I shout, "Where are my children?!"

No one responds. People stare at me in confusion. I run to the home next door, leaving the chaos in my front yard behind me. The neighbors are watching the chaos in the cul-de-sac from their front porch, fearful and upset that something has happened to the nice new family in the neighborhood. They don't know where my children are, so I run to the next home. Those neighbors are on their front porch, holding each other. They don't have an answer either, but they say I should check the next house.

All the neighbors are standing on their front lawns or steps, except for Dan and Michelle. All the lights are on in their house, and I see a lot of people inside. I run up their steps and after a quick knock on their door, it flies open. Dan stands there; his eyes are red and welled up. I see Kevin and Seantay; there is horror in their young eyes. They come screaming to me. I fall to my knees in the entryway of this home that has been my children's sanctuary for the last thirty minutes. Screaming, they tell me what happened, with floods of salty tears soaking their faces and shirts. I hold them tight, not knowing what to say. I just hold my children and tell them I'm glad they're safe and assure them they did the right thing.

Later, I learn the kids had been sitting together in the front room watching the movie *A Bug's Life*. To this day, they won't watch that movie. While they were watching the movie, Canyon had gone out of the room and into our bedroom. He had been gone a short time when they heard what they thought sounded like a dresser falling to the floor. It startled them because it was loud and shook the house. They thought it was strange, but they kept watching the movie. When Seantay and Kevin heard the same explosive crack of thunder again minutes later, both jumped up and ran to my bedroom door. Instinctively, they knew something was wrong. They left Spencer and Sierra in front of the movie and ran toward the sound. Our bedroom door was locked. They called for Canyon but there was no answer. They yelled for him again, but still there was no answer.

Worried for her older brother, Seantay found a hairpin, put it into the doorknob, and opened the door. And then,

# The Phone Call

the innocence of my children's young lives was rent from them forever as they stepped into a world of horror and took in a scene no one should ever have to see.

They left the room, ran to my office, and slammed the door shut, both screaming and jumping up and down as they tried to call me. When I answered, they both tried to tell me what had happened and how they needed me, but I was gone. I had hung up on them when they needed me to be there more than ever. In a hysterical panic, they called Michelle, our neighbor, for help.

Michelle left her home and her own children to run to the rescue of my children. She gathered them up, called 911, and hurried them back to her home across the cul-de-sac. They never stopped screaming, and I can only imagine the horror that entered our dear new friend's home that evening.

Still holding my children, a woman I don't recognize comes up to me. She introduces herself as a trauma specialist for children from the city police department. She tells me she has been talking with the children, and all they need right now is their parents. She says she will be back to talk with me later. Dan and Michelle are standing close by, their faces stained with tears. Spencer is in another room, apparently oblivious to what has happened, and another neighbor holds Sierra. Sierra, just past five months old, is too young to comprehend the situation, and she seems to be fine. Seantay and Kevin are not.

We cry together for several minutes before someone helps Cologne to the front door of our friend's home. She enters with a couple of police officers helping her walk. She embraces us, and the four of us cry together in each other's arms. Temporarily, the chaos outside is shut out. There is nothing we can do. I have only one task: Somehow, I need to comfort my horrifically traumatized family.

Several people go in and out of the home. A detective asks me whether he can talk to me privately. We walk into the dining room. He tells me what he found upon entering our home. He explains, as compassionately as possible, why we should not go into our home, at least not until our bedroom has been cleaned by professionals.

He tells me of the gun Canyon had found in my closet and of the two shots that had taken place. He asks me whether I want him to destroy the gun. I quickly agree. He tells me he'll be writing up a report, and I can read it later.

"I'm terribly sorry for your loss," he says. "This has been extremely difficult on all of us this evening. It's obvious you have a wonderful family and that there's a lot of love in your home. All my men want you to know how sorry they are."

Three other officers come in to talk to me that evening to let me know they'll be there for me if I need them. Everything is such a blur, and yet I feel the compassion all around us. People want to come in, hug us, and give us their love and condolences, but at the same time, they respect the rawness of our trauma and give us some space. Those who were there that evening share a tremendous amount of heartfelt compassion and love.

None of us can breathe very well, and we've cried to the point of dehydration and exhaustion. Our friends make up an area in their home for us to sleep. They inflate an air mattress, bring in some blankets, and then leave us to ourselves to mourn and figure out how to sleep. A

# The Phone Call

doctor friend of ours brings us some sleeping pills. We're surrounded by thoughtful compassion.

We want it all to go away and be a bad dream. The pain is beyond description as we miss our son and older brother. Our chests hurt from the painful tightness, our bodies are exhausted, and we can barely see out of our swollen red eyes.

---

One minute our lives were just about perfect. Things were going so well. We were the picture-perfect family who had overcome significant problems and were an example to those who knew us. We thought the storm was over, but it hadn't even begun.

As if struck by a sudden tidal wave, our lives were upside down. We were left drowning in a murky mess of confusion and sorrow. We found ourselves gasping for breath and reaching for anything to grab onto in the dirty, debris-filled water rushing over us. A rush of current swept us away from all we knew and loved dearly. We're sure we can never survive this pain.

# CANYON GRIEVES WITH GRANDMA

EVERYONE HAD LEFT FOR THE EVENING and our neighbor's home had grown quiet. Our hosts had gone to bed, though I don't imagine sleep came quickly. It was late in the night. Cologne, the children, and I were still huddled together in the dim light of the front living room. There was no noise other than our soft crying and sniffles. We no longer had the strength or hydration to pour out more tears.

Our broken hearts were alone together for the first time after the horror of what had occurred. We needed to go to sleep, but each of us was carrying a heart that couldn't stop aching. No one said a thing and no one needed to; we just sat there and hurt in silence, wondering whether what we felt was real, or just a bad dream.

I suggested we say a prayer together as a family. It seemed like the right thing to do to help comfort our pain in some way. We all desperately needed help that no one on earth could provide. I didn't know what else to do. Everyone agreed, so I offered the prayer.

Time seemed to stand still. I could hardly breathe, let alone speak. It took me some time to find my voice. The sentences that came out of my mouth were short because I didn't know what to say. I didn't know how to pray at that dreadful moment. My throat had a lump in it as if I was trying to swallow a tennis ball. I could hardly see out of my eyes because they were so swollen from crying.

I thanked the Lord for our Canyon, for all he meant to us. I told Him how much we loved Canyon, how much we cared about him, and how much we would miss him. I asked Him for strength and I asked Him to bless my children, to comfort their hearts and to give Cologne and me the strength to take care of our family. I asked Him to help me to know what to do. I asked Him to help us understand and to take away some of our pain. I asked Him to help us know what to do for each other. I didn't know what else to say.

In that silence, as I prayed, in my mind I saw my loving mother, who'd passed away from cancer at the early age of forty-seven, standing before me with her arms around my son Canyon. She held him peacefully before us, and with heads reverently bowed, the two of them joined us in prayer. I saw their faces as they stood just in front of us. She was consoling him, and I saw his pain.

Kevin had been sitting on my lap, tightly pulled into my chest. I felt his confusion and pain. He had just gone through the horror of finding his older brother dead in his parents' bedroom, the walls sprayed with Canyon's own blood. But just when I saw my mother holding Canyon, I felt Kevin relax.

When I closed the prayer, Kevin stretched up, tickled my ear with his lips and the warm breath from his mouth, and whispered with a voice that cut through my soul.

"Daddy, did you see them?" I knew what he meant, and I knew we had seen them together, but I asked him anyway.

"What?"

"Did you see Grandma and Canyon?" he repeated.

I tried not to cry, but I couldn't hold it back. And as the flood of tears broke forth again, Kevin cried with me. We held each other tightly, and I tried to get enough air to speak.

"Yes, son . . . I saw them."

"Canyon looked sad, Daddy, but I'm happy he's with Grandma. She'll take good care of him."

"Yes, Kevin," I said. "She sure will."

Kevin was just a baby, eighteen months old, when my mother had passed. Yet somehow, he knew who was with Canyon and recognized her as Grandma.

As we continued to hold each other, the tears didn't stop. We were consoled by what we had just experienced. Our hearts felt softer, but we still hurt. Cologne and Seantay hadn't had the same experience, but they were comforted to hear about it. It gave us all just enough peace finally to go to sleep.

## SEAN M. FLEMING

# THE LETTER

Soon after Canyon was gone, a close friend suggested I write Canyon a letter. Here is the letter I wrote him on December 11, 2001, just days after his death. I read this letter at his funeral.

Dear Canyon,

I struggle for breath. I don't know what to do. I feel such a loss. I have lost you, my son, my eldest son. There is a big hole in my soul that needs to be filled. I can't get the next breath; it feels as if the breath has been sucked out of me. It's a crushing pain, as if a large boulder has rolled onto my chest. I know I need to be strong for your mother, brothers, and sisters. I promise I will learn from the mistakes of our past. I will live life as though I have but little time left with every member of our family.

I would give everything I have for just one minute with you. One minute to say goodbye, to give you another hug, and to tell you once more that I love you. You were plucked away from me before we had a chance to do all the things we wanted to. Even so, I am grateful for the short time I had you, one of God's finest sons, in my care while on this earth.

I am thankful for the memories we do have. Yes, I wanted to do more. I wanted to say many things we didn't have a chance to talk about. Still, we had a lot of fun together. You were young and just starting to become a man. You were growing into yourself and starting to do things that made me proud. I can't express how sorry I am to lose you.

Those little things you did—at the time I thought were just plain goofy—were part of what made you wonderful. They made you unique. They made you impossible to replace. I will ache to go skiing with you. I will ache to go hiking or fishing with you. I will ache to watch you play hockey, and I'm sorry I didn't go to every game. If I can ever stand to go to karate again, I will ache to have you there with me.

I hurt for your friends. Did they really know what they had? I see their pain and realize I don't know what they had, either. But I know what I had. I had an amazing and obedient son. I had a son who was caring, feeling, and had a tender spirit, a son who liked to be with his family, who liked to spend time playing and working with his dad. I had a son who thought deeply and taught us so much. I had a son who loved his family with all his heart and would do anything for them. I had a son who respected his mother and was tender and caring with his brothers and sisters. I had a son who made mistakes and learned from them. I'm sorry some mistakes don't come with second chances. I would do anything to give you that second chance.

I feel no anger for what you did. I only feel pain and loss. I know you loved your family too much to have made that decision in whole consciousness. I know you wouldn't have wanted the turn of events that happened afterwards to have occurred. You loved Seantay and Kevin far too much to have wanted to leave them with the aftermath. I know you loved your father and mother far too much to have meant to cause them such great pain.

Canyon, I cannot remember a time that you ever yelled at me in anger. As you held your little sister, Sierra, that evening close to your breast, her cheek next to yours, your smile, which distinctly made you who you are, was full of love. I know you wouldn't have wanted to leave her behind the way you did. Your willingness to help with Spencer was tender. He depended on you so much. You knew he loved and needed you. You were always willing to help. You knew your father and mother loved you. I believe you are grieving just as we are. I will always hate what happened, but I forgive you, Canyon, my son. I forgive you. I look forward to embracing you again.

With all my love,

# THE SILENT DOOR

*"If we will be ready and quiet enough,*
*we shall find compensation in every disappointment."*

~ Henry David Thoreau

THERE IS A DOORWAY IN LIFE WE ALL NOTICE. We pretend we don't notice it until someone we know passes through it and doesn't return. Even as a kid, I knew it was there, but I didn't want to acknowledge it. The first funeral I remember going to was my Nana's.

Nana was my great-grandmother. She had red hair like me (or so everyone said) before it turned white. She was tiny, frail, and had a special place in my heart because she made candy. Her father had owned a candy store in Boise, Idaho, and she grew up making candy. I have a strong affinity for English toffee because of my Nana's incredible talent. I remember thinking she must be magic to be able to make such incredible treats. I didn't know anyone else who made candy. Everyone talked about Nana's secret recipes. She lived in a little candy pink house, and when we visited, she always had something sweet for us to enjoy.

Nana's ninetieth birthday was a hoot. I remember how bright she was that day, joking with everyone and wanting to eat my grandma's lemon meringue pie. Soon after that birthday party, the doorway I refused to acknowledge opened for Nana, and she passed through it. She took her magic recipes with her. She was gone and I was numb. Even then, I still refused to acknowledge that doorway. I didn't understand it. I was young and only wanted to think about life. To me, Nana's death just happened and was over. I didn't give it much thought. I didn't want to acknowledge that my Nana was gone. No one else talked about it much either, at least not around me.

It wasn't until I got older that I realized what an unhealthy relationship I had with death and my understanding of death. It wasn't until I lost my own mother that I stared at the doorway and really wanted to know what was on the other side.

Losing someone close to you takes you nearer to the silent doorway of death, a mysterious passageway we all must pass through. This final act of our mortal lives can cause great anxiety. We're not sure what, if anything, exists beyond that doorway. It's a mystery to which we all seem to need an answer. We've been taught different things by those we know, love, and respect. Opinions vary greatly. Some have gone beyond that doorway and returned, and although some of their stories resonate with what we have been taught, others differ. No one has definitive knowledge, only memories and faith, and there are no witnesses to what anyone experienced.

Logically, it would be more helpful if two people passed

through this doorway at the same time, witnessed the exact same things, and returned to tell us all. But this hasn't happened. Though many have similar experiences, no one has the same experience at the same time.

I have been drawn close to this doorway many times since I have lost several people very close to me—besides my precious son. I lost my mother when she was just forty-seven years old, and both sets of grandparents, whom I loved and adored. My father's parents seemed almost immortal as I was growing up. They never seemed to age. I was very close to them. I also lost one of my favorite cousins when he was a young adult, and I lost two uncles and a couple of dear friends. These loved ones were people who were important to me. They were people to whom I felt close. They left me wondering where they'd gone.

In some ways, I feel like the little water bug below the surface waiting for that knowledge, from a deal struck with a close friend, who will come back and give me the information that will enlighten my understanding. No one comes back, however, and there is precious little information for my hungry soul. We need hope in order to listen and move forward with our lives when such questions and loss loom overhead.

One thing is certain. All of us must go through this doorway. And witnessing those close to us passing through it causes us to question. We each question differently, depending on our background and faith, but in general, we question the meaning of life. "What is it all about? Does God really exist?" we ask. "What is beyond that doorway?" and, "What am I doing with the life I've got left?"

In that respect, death may be the single greatest invention by a creator in this life, because it causes us to question on such a deep level. It causes us to search on a level beyond the physical body, to hear the answers our souls yearn to hear. They are questions that have haunted man since the beginning of time, questions we still ask despite all the times they have been asked over the millennia. They are questions that appear to have no definitive answers.

The truth is that we'll never know what lies beyond death's door until we pass through it ourselves. I once heard someone say, "You can't truly live until you have learned to die." This statement has stayed with me over the years because I believe there's some truth to it. Until you overcome your fear of death, you are not truly able to live with the passion it takes to break through the barriers in your mind. I'm referring to barriers that have been passed down through centuries of ancestors, none of whom knew what is beyond that doorway, but they came up with all kinds of stories to explain it. When you've been taught there is life beyond this doorway, it can be comforting, but it adds to your curiosity and even your need to question whether those beliefs are true.

I know there's only one way to find out and have my questions answered for certain, and that is to pass beyond this doorway myself and find out, finally, the truth of it all. However, there is one obvious problem with this discovery technique. It can't be on my time line. Once I pass through that doorway, there's no coming back. It's a one-way ticket. No round-trip passes available. So until then, I must submit to a choice of how I'm going to live. I choose to live with love and joy and to experience life to its fullest. Nana knows, my mother knows, and Canyon knows, but I still get to wonder. Eventually, I'll find out what's beyond the door, but what's the hurry? People who want and need me are still here. I can still bless lives here, including my own.

If a Supreme Being exists who is the author and finisher of all of this, and I strongly agree there is, then I ask myself whether there is a purpose in this dilemma of not knowing. The answer I enjoy (because it resonates with my soul and my belief system) is that it's the perfect trial. There is a Divine order to why we come into this life not remembering anything prior, and why we later pass through that doorway, exiting this life without a return ticket. Still, many people believe this life is all there is because we seek for evidence to confirm our belief systems and often find little or none. Or do we? What sort of evidence are we open to? What type of clues are we willing to listen to? I believe there are clues all around us.

Hope has kept those before us pressing forward. Hope is the magical starting place of movement. It is the seed that, if planted, grows into faith.

Again, my purpose is not to say that everyone must believe in a Higher Power. I share my belief in one because it has been such a critical component of my survival. I believe that believing in something bigger than ourselves makes us stronger and gives us hope.

Hope is the first component for dealing with the grief of losing a loved one. Without hope for something, you have nothing. Hopelessness is an empty hollow feeling that offers no chance of answering the questions of your soul.

Have hope. Start with hope that life wasn't wasted, that the time you had with your loved one was for a purpose. Have hope that the pain will go away and you will be able to breathe again. Hope that your heart will heal, that you will be able to move again. Have hope that spring will come, and you will be able to enjoy the beauty of life again. Hope there is a purpose for this life, and hope you will see your loved one again. Hope that where your loved ones are is a wonderful place where they are happy. Hope they are flying as the new golden dragonfly, preparing and waiting to greet you when the time is right. Hope that by moving forward and fulfilling your purpose in life, others will gain more from the loss than the loss itself. Hope you can and will be the light that gives others hope and makes their burdens seem lighter.

# DANDELIONS IN THE OUTFIELD

*"When you eventually see through the veils
to how things really are,
you will keep saying again and again,
this is certainly not like we thought it was."*

~ Jalal al-Din Rumi

T-BALL WAS CANYON'S FIRST ATTEMPT AT SPORTS when he was about four years old. It didn't go so well. He loved the part where he got to play with friends and run around, but he didn't get what all the fuss was about when it came to beating the other team. The competitive aspect was simply unimportant to him. The coach assigned Canyon to center field, probably because the chance of a youngster hitting clear out into center field was remote.

Canyon wasn't particularly slow or clumsy; he just wasn't concerned enough with winning. He simply wanted to play. In theory, sports for kids this age are just for fun, and it doesn't really matter who wins. We just want the kids to have a good time, right? Well, we all know what actually happens. Parents yell and scream, trying to be the best cheerleaders possible, and sometimes they get a little bit carried away. Parents, in their exuberance, often make the mistake of caring more than their kids do about who wins.

Then there are those granddaddy mistakes at which everyone can't help but laugh. I'll admit, I couldn't help but laugh at some of those innocent mistakes myself, even though the kids probably didn't see the humor. I remember one of those moments clearly with my son.

---

It's a bright sunny day. There's not a cloud in the sky. The grass is green and the score is tied. The bases are loaded. It's common in T-Ball for the bases to be loaded, and home runs are uncommon. But it's easier to make a home run when the center fielder is busy picking dandelions and ignoring the ball. Canyon has been picking them for a while and has a handful of them. It's obvious he's enjoying himself because he doesn't hear me yell.

"Canyon! Look up! Here comes the ball!" My face is flushed red with embarrassment.

Not only does my son not see the ball, but he is facing the other direction! He is actually sitting down with his legs spread apart on the ground and his mitt beside him.

The ball rolls right up to his little feet and stops. We're all screaming at the top of our lungs, "Canyon, get the ball!" Finally, he looks up and notices everyone yelling at him. He must be confused about why we're getting so excited because the first thing he does is wave happily to everyone with a sweet, open smile on his face. Then he notices the right and left fielders running toward him for the ball. With their shirts too big, and their little legs trying to hurry, they look as if they might trip on their jerseys, but they are determined that, if Canyon isn't going to get the ball, they will.

Finally, Canyon spots the ball and seems to realize what's going on. Leaving his glove behind, he heads for the ball, then bends over and picks it up. But in the process, he drops a couple of his precious dandelions. He quickly prioritizes by putting the ball down in order to pick up the dandelions he dropped. He carefully returns them to his hand where they were so perfectly placed before. Only when they are rearranged does he pick up the ball again. Everyone is hollering even louder for him to throw the ball. The runners are running over home plate one at a time, their little legs carrying them gleefully to their cheering teammates. The batter is rounding second base, his coach and team parents screaming for him to run faster.

Canyon is right-handed, but he has the ball in his left hand because dandelions occupy his right hand. He pulls the ball back with a straight arm behind him. His tongue is hanging out of his mouth. He gives the ball a soft underhand roll, sending it awkwardly toward first base instead of to the catcher where it's needed. Everyone sighs in resignation, and some laugh. The first baseman runs for the ball, but the runner is nearly home. All the runners end up crossing the plate. Canyon can't figure out why everyone is so excited.

He never lets go of the flowers, and at the end of the game, he takes them to his mother. His sweet young face is beaming when he hands her the drooping little bouquet. I don't think it matters at all to him that the other team has won. He's achieved his objective. He's gotten those flowers safely to his mother, and for him, that's really the most important thing he could do. He is proud of himself, and Cologne is beaming like a proud mother and letting him be the true champion he is.

---

Canyon had it right all along. To him, his gesture of love in bringing a handful of weedy flowers to his mother was infinitely more important than winning any game.

That childlike wisdom Canyon had was the kind of thing I didn't realize when I had him with me. Now I understand it, and I thank him for that lesson. It is the little moments, the precious moments with those we love, that mean everything—everything else is relatively unimportant. I try to keep this lesson in my heart. I want to live each day with my eyes open a little wider to the precious moments we often too easily ignore or discard as unimportant or even annoying. Too often, the things we think matter, don't actually matter at all. Too often, the things we don't pay enough attention to are the most precious gems of our lives, if we could only recognize them.

# LITTLE THINGS

*"A man's house burns down. The smoking wreckage represents only a ruined home that was dear through years of use and pleasant associations. By and by, as the days and weeks go on, first he misses this, then that, then the other thing. And when he casts about for it he finds that it was in that house. Always it is an essential—there was but one of its kind. It cannot be replaced. It was in that house. It is irrevocably lost. It will be years before the tale of lost essentials is complete, and not till then can he truly know the magnitude of his disaster."*

~ Mark Twain

When you lose a loved one, it's the little things you remember and miss. The quirks of personality and the memory of shared experiences that seemed insignificant at the time are all too precious once someone is gone. Most memories make me happy, but others sneak up on me and surprise me with tremendous feelings of loss. I try to focus on the happy memories of Canyon. It seems appropriate to focus on the beauty and fullness he brought into our lives. He brought joy to my life in ways I never expected.

Canyon was a sweet child. He was bright and lively, yet very low maintenance. He had a hypnotic, peaceful way about him, but he had an insatiable appetite to learn and asked questions constantly. One of these innocent questions still makes me laugh. When Seantay was an infant, Cologne pumped breast milk to feed her since Seantay couldn't nurse because of a cleft pallet. Canyon sometimes served as an extra set of hands to help his mother out when I was gone.

We were eating fried chicken one evening for dinner when I asked Cologne what piece of chicken she wanted. She said, "A leg, please." Canyon looked at her inquisitively. He paused, spent some time studying the piece of chicken on his plate, and asked, "What part of the chicken do I have?" Cologne replied, "The breast." He looked at Cologne, gave a little scrunch to his nose, and looked again at the chicken on his plate. He looked at her again, then looked at me, and down at his chicken again. "Huh," was his puzzled response as he continued to look at his chicken, still with his scrunched nose.

He picked it up, studied it, and turned it in his hands to see both sides. He picked at it with his fingers and pulled some of the breading off. Then he looked up at Cologne and asked, "Where's the nipple?" We laughed, and Canyon laughed with us as Cologne told him chickens don't have nipples. "Oh, that's good," he said, then took a big bite of his chicken as if it had never really mattered.

# Little Things

Canyon had the ability to talk to anyone, even when he was young. He'd strike up a conversation with anyone we were near. When I was growing up, I was taught not to talk to strangers, so I wanted the same for my children's safety. Well, I had the hardest time teaching this concept to Canyon. People were good to him because he was so cute. He loved to talk to adults, even more than other children, because adults were more interesting and talked about things he wanted to learn about.

As a child, I loved hiking with my father. I would follow behind him, trying to step exactly where he stepped, and in a small way, to be just like him. I remember taking Canyon hiking when he was about five. There I was, years later, an adult with my own son looking up at me as if I were that same infallible being I had once seen in my father. With the enthusiasm only the very young can muster, Canyon followed right behind me, trying hard to make his footsteps land exactly in mine.

I wish I had been more aware of how his young little mind worked. For example, I was not very understanding when it came to how distracted he could be during sports. His mind needed to be stimulated on a different level than sports provided him. For Canyon, the basic problem with sports was that they weren't interesting to him. Competition wasn't important to him. Running after a ball just didn't get him charged up like it did with other children.

Many times I was embarrassed by his indifference and wished he would try harder. *He's fully capable. Why does this seem to be such a problem?* I'd wonder. I spent time trying to encourage him and help him do better, but it just didn't happen. From soccer to basketball, he tried nearly everything, but never for more than a year or two.

After the year or two had passed, I'd say, "It's okay, Canyon. You gave it a try. That's what matters."

"Yeah, Dad. I gave it a try."

He was good at a lot of other things, though. He loved problem-solving games and puzzles. He started beating me at chess when he was only eight years old, which frustrated me because of my competitive personality. I didn't need to go easy on him because even when I did my very best, he won. I played extra slowly to give myself time to strategize. I was sure each time would be the time I'd win. I was finally going to beat him, yet he still won every time, like it was the easiest thing in the world to do. "It's okay, Daddy," he would say when he saw my genuine disappointment. "You gave it a try. That's what matters. Maybe you can beat me next time." I wonder whether he enjoyed the irony of having to encourage me. I hope he did.

As with all of my children, Canyon enriched my life by giving me the opportunity to love someone uniquely different from myself. Even though Canyon and I were not connected genetically, as our family grew, my relationship with Canyon seemed no different than if we were biologically related.

Canyon loved life and it showed. That contradicts the way he died, I know. As much as he loved life, why would he kill himself? I don't have an answer to that. All I know is that sometimes people do things in a moment of confusion or weakness that does not necessarily reflect who they are. The Canyon I knew loved people, and so many people loved

# Little Things

him. He had a way of making people feel special. He just had a gift.

He was as good a son as any father could have wished to have. He didn't always keep his room clean, and he didn't always take the garbage out when we asked. Sometimes he teased his younger brother and sisters and got in trouble for it, but we all learned from those experiences about how to be better people.

I have always been competitive. Canyon, on the other hand, loved computers, video games, math, and music. Like any father, I couldn't understand some aspects of Canyon's personality and preferences. I knew nothing about music. Just like with chess, I couldn't beat him at any video game to save my life, and believe me, I tried. As a confident optimist, every time we played video games together, I actually thought I had a chance of winning. Canyon must have had a difficult time holding back laughter at my lack of skills and false sense of hope when it came to video games, but he was too kind to rub it in.

Canyon taught himself to play the piano because he was frustrated with piano lessons. The formal instruction seemed to hold him back. He had a natural gift that didn't want to be confined by systems and theory. I remember listening to him teach himself to play a popular Yanni song by listening to part of the song on the stereo downstairs, then running upstairs to the piano to identify the right keys by ear. It didn't take him long to master the entire song. Having no talent for music myself, I was completely amazed to see that "playing by ear" is indeed humanly possible. He played that Yanni song for us often. In my mind, I can still hear him playing that song, with a victorious smile of satisfaction and pride.

Canyon and I participated in scouting, which meant spending time together camping and earning merit badges. He eventually received his Eagle Scout award, which was something that made us both proud.

As Canyon grew, his athletic abilities changed. He took to skiing and mountain biking. He loved to spend time on the mountain with me. We were in karate together and he later discovered he loved hockey.

He was responsible and kind with his brothers and sisters. They probably aren't aware of how much he suffered on their behalf by being the first one to teach his father and mother how to raise children. His siblings had a much easier time as my wife and I became more skilled as parents. Cologne and I did our best to raise him with love and respect, and I have no serious regrets as his father.

However, I didn't completely know my son. There was a gracious and deep side to him I never fully recognized until he died. His funeral was packed. I can only hope to have that many people care enough about me. It was overwhelming and inspiring. From that day until weeks after, I had a new glimpse into how much of a man my son was. He was no respecter of persons, meaning he didn't play favorites but liked everyone. He genuinely tried to make people feel important, and he succeeded. For weeks after his death, we received letters from people who had known and loved him. We received letters from kids I wouldn't have wanted my son to hang around, to kids I didn't even think he knew. We have a couple of three-ring binders full of these letters telling stories of my son. To this day, I can't read through them without getting emotional.

Sometimes when we're close to people and accustomed to them, it is difficult to recognize the incredible treasures they truly are. I recognized my son as a treasure. It wasn't until I lost that treasure that I started looking around for the things I missed and realized much of them were irreplaceable, priceless.

# RED-SHELL SAND

*"I pointed to the sky to show you the moon,
but all you saw was the tip of my finger."*

~ African Proverb

---

My family is walking along Anini Beach on the north shore of Kauai. The coarse sand softly crunches under our sandals as Cologne and I walk together along this romantic beach, a short stretch of paradise. The breakers out beyond the reef caress our ears with a calm soothing sound. The sun is setting and the pink light reflects across the still, calm waters sheltered by the reef. The rougher waves further out can't get past the massive fence of coral. Nothing interrupts this water. The rocks that break the surface stand like sentinels in the pink glass-like water.

In these still waters, two men with long spears wade, knee-deep, a couple of hundred feet out in the water. The silhouettes move gracefully, framed by the light beyond, as they hunt for octopuses. I watch in eager curiosity as nothing happens. Their still, calm wading is hypnotic as they drag their shadows behind them. It barely disturbs the glass effect of the water's pink surface. The brown lava cliffs to our left rise above us over the palms on the shoreline. A long branch of a banyan tree stretches out horizontally over the sand, forming a naturally perfect bench.

We sit on a strong branch that barely moves under our weight. Together, Cologne and I enjoy the sunset. Big, puffy clouds are stacked high in the sky. They look almost hand-painted as they reflect the pink and orange lights from the sunset onto everything around them.

I am completely relaxed and committed to enjoying this perfect moment in time. The thought occurs to me that I may have discovered one of the most beautiful places on earth, and at the very least, one of the most peaceful. I wonder how life could get any better than this. I realize how blessed I am. There is a smile on my face as I cradle my wife close to me in my arms.

I see a pretty shell nestled up against a rock a few feet away and curiously hop off my bench to retrieve it. As I pick it up and return to Cologne, I brush some of the sand off for her to see its beauty. The sand sticks to my fingers as I try to brush it off. The sand itself is colored in lovely shades of champagne and red wine. It has almost a ruby-red sparkle to it.

Then I notice some of the sand is not really sand; the red specks are actually very tiny snail-like shells. Some are bright and some dull, but all are exquisitely minute shells. I am so fascinated that I almost forget the original shell as I excitedly show Cologne how the sand is full of little

# Red-Shell Sand

wonders. She smiles, but she is not as fascinated as I am. I've been distracted from our romantic embrace, which is more important to her, and am asked to return.

The next day, we walk along a row of crafters' booths in a little art fair in Kapaa, enjoying the different arts and crafts people have made and are selling. A beaded necklace catches my eye on a white linen-covered table. An older Asian couple sits behind the table. I ask whether I can pick up one of the necklaces. When I do, I recognize the beads are small red shells that have been strung tightly together in bunches. The couple has made different styles of necklaces, bracelets, and hairpieces, all from those small shells no more than the size of birdseed. The white table is covered with many of these differently colored creations of reds and amber. Each one is made up of thousands of strung shells separated into similar colors. They are exquisite and very expensive, which is understandable considering all the time that must have been involved in making them.

I realize these shells are the very same type of shell I had seen the evening before. I ask the elderly couple how they got all the little shells and where they found them. They say they gathered them from a secret beach, sorted them into similar shades, and strung them together. I notice a look of pride in their faces as they talk about their tiny treasures while they are cautious not to let out too much information about their secret beach.

My daughter, Seantay, thinks the necklaces are captivating and asks whether she can have one. I am too stunned by the price to agree. But after we are a distance away from the elderly couple's booth, I notice my daughter's disappointed face. I lean down to tell her "the secret"—that I know where they got the shells and that we can go there ourselves and gather enough to make her a bracelet or necklace.

Seantay gasps in delight. "Really? How do you know, Daddy?"

"Well," I say, savoring her happy response, "I found some last night as your mother and I were walking along the beach."

Her initial surprise and delight quickly turn into questions. How do we know we can find enough? How do we know we can string them like that? How long will it take? All great questions I tactfully avoid.

She wisely notes, "I don't know, Daddy; it might be worth it just to buy one now." I don't hear the wisdom in her voice at that moment. Instead, I convince myself, and my daughter, that my plan is better.

Two hours later, we are on the beach with a jar in hand to hold our bounty. After quite some time of walking up and down the beach, we find a place that seems to have a little greater concentration of coarser red specks in the sand. We're excited to plop ourselves down on the "jackpot" beach and begin sifting through the sand. "Here's one!" I shout with excitement.

"I found one too!" she says happily.

Plink, plink go our first two shells in the jar. Many plinks follow, and we are excited. The shells are all over the place, like stars in the sky. Unfortunately, not every shell is whole. Some are broken and crushed. It's harder to find whole ones we can use than I had guessed it would be.

# Red-Shell Sand

Canyon and Kevin are there too, generously helping us. They are almost as excited about our new discovery and help us make a game of it. After about thirty minutes, we have the bottom of the jar speckled with the tiny little shells, but we probably only have fifty or so in total. Because of their smallness, fifty shells will not be nearly enough to make any kind of creation remotely similar to what we had seen earlier in the day—not even close.

Seantay is gracious enough to avoid saying, "I told you so," but her expression says it all. "Boy, this is going to take a long time, Daddy," she notes. I do not respond, but I do ask myself how much of our vacation I really want to spend picking out specks of sand on a beach when I could be doing other things. However, for now, collecting shells feels like the most valuable thing I can be doing. For a moment, time stands still as it had the evening before. I am spending some precious discovery time with my children, but I certainly question my patience in keeping up this task long enough to keep the commitment I've made to Seantay.

And then, as if reading my mind, Canyon and Kevin lose all interest. The shells have become too common to "ooh" and "ahh" over. They head out to hunt for coconuts to float in the water. Seantay, as the potential recipient of the treasure, is a little more determined. But after an hour and a half of picking through the sand, her excitement has started to fizzle out as well.

"Wow," I say in a feeble attempt to admit to being wrong without actually having to admit it. "This isn't as easy as I thought it would be."

"Yeah, it's taking a long time," she says, "but they're

everywhere. It's kind of strange, how earlier we hardly found any, and now they're all over the place." At this point, we might have one-hundred-and-fifty of these precious little shells at the bottom of our jar. We might be able to make a thin little single strand bracelet, but that pales in comparison to what we saw at the art fair.

Just as I am starting to regret my decision because I can no longer see a successful outcome, Seantay looks up at me, and smiles. "I sure like spending time with you, Daddy," she exclaims. "You're the greatest."

I feel a little better in spite of my lack of judgment. Just then, Kevin and Canyon run up the beach to ask whether we can go back to the condo and go in the pool. Seantay looks like she's trying to hold back some disappointment. When I ask them to give us a little more time, they run off into the palm trees to find some more coconuts.

I look at her and say, "What do you say we go back and buy one of those finished necklaces at the art fair from the nice lady?"

"Really?!"

"Sure. I really thought we could do this, but now I'm starting to wonder."

"Can we keep the ones we found?" she asks.

"Of course," I say. "We've worked hard for these." As I hold the jar up to the light and examine our prize, she smiles a big proud grin.

When we return to the art fair, we are disappointed to find that everyone is packing up and leaving. Some artists have already left, including the elderly couple. We ask a passerby whether the fair will be there tomorrow.

# Red-Shell Sand

"No, but it will be back next week," he replies.

We have already been in Kauai three days and are only staying a week. We'll be flying home before the next arts and crafts fair. We've missed our window of opportunity. I know Seantay is disappointed, but she is gracious to me.

"It's okay, Daddy; we can get one next time we come to Kauai."

"Sure," I say a bit reluctantly, not knowing when or if we'll ever be back. I know she's thinking the same thing, but is just being kind.

"I think it's cool how you knew where to find the shells and that we went and found so many by ourselves. That was fun, Daddy. Thank you."

Seantay, always good at seeing the positive in everything, continues, "They're kind of not as 'wow' now that we know where they are and how to get them. I don't know how bad I really want one anyway. I feel special because you wanted to get me one and that's enough."

---

I appreciate her forgiveness, but I feel less forgiving of myself for being a stubborn tightwad. Live and learn, they say. I'm grateful Seantay was willing to let it be a happy memory for us when it could have just as easily been a heartbreaking one.

It is curious how we go through life not noticing little things, but once we become aware of something, one little thing, a whole new awareness of possibility opens before us. I'd been on that beach several times before and had never noticed it was filled with those intricate little shells. It was just sand to me, nothing more. Then, in a moment of greater awareness and grateful appreciation, I looked closer and a whole world of treasure opened up. At first glance, I felt Seantay and I had wasted an afternoon collecting too few shells to do anything with, but when I looked closer, I saw what a meaningful and memorable afternoon it had been, laughing and talking with my daughter. That was my treasure and hers.

Looking back at the experience with the red shells, I can't help but see them as a metaphor for the little things we could easily miss in life. So many precious little things are just beneath our feet.

I learned so much about Canyon after losing him. It wasn't until he was gone that I was able to notice all the little joys that left with him, all the little things I took for granted when he was with us.

Sometimes the precious gems in life are right under our feet, and because we are familiar with them or we don't recognize them, we trample them in our well-intentioned haste to get through life or "get ahead." Later, most people learn that in the end, getting matters less than being present for your children. What is imperative—what does matter—is making space for precious moments with your children, taking time to appreciate their uniqueness, and making sure they know you love them.

# THE ACCIDENT

Just before I fell asleep the evening of Canyon's death, I saw him in my mind, as if a dream, but real. He said he was sorry. It was so sincere and heartfelt that I actually felt some of the pain and sorrow he was feeling. The impression came strong and clear. With it came a glimpse of what might have happened earlier that evening when he shot himself. It happened quickly in my mind, but it was real and undeniable. I saw the curiosity of a young man who was looking for Christmas presents in his parents' closet and instead found an old rifle he had never seen before. In his searching through boxes, he also found old bullet rounds and wondered whether they were for the same gun. He loaded the gun. Then, curious and playing around, he chambered one of the shells. The gun was armed and ready. He was familiar with guns, but not the old WWII rifle I'd planned to restore. During his inspection of it, the gun misfired. The sound of the explosion echoed through the master bedroom and bathroom, connected as one open room with a large vaulted ceiling connecting the two. The gun recoiled in his hands and hurt him. It was unexpected, a mistake, and the experience of the terrible sound, getting hurt, and damaging our room, scared him so badly that he lost his reasoning mind. Confused, conflicted, and concerned about the consequences, he went through the motions of how he could make it all stop. And in a moment of emotional chaos, he finished his mortal life without completely knowing he had.

I saw him, in spirit, standing above his limp body, trying to fix the mistake he'd made. He didn't fully realize he was dead at first and wanted desperately to correct things. I saw his pain and anguish as he realized he was dead and what he had done. I saw and felt the confusion in his mind at how quickly it had happened and how he had never meant to kill himself. I saw him hurt badly when his brother and sister came into the room, and when there was nothing he could do about it, how he cried over their fear and trauma of finding such a horrific sight. I saw how much he regretted that he had hurt everyone, and how he hadn't completely meant to do it. I understood, how, in a moment, he had lost his mind and made a mistake he couldn't rectify or restore. I heard his apology, and as I cried for him, I forgave him. The last words I said that evening as I fell asleep were, "I forgive you, Canyon."

# The Accident

## Twenty-Two Years Earlier . . .

When I was fourteen, I was in my bedroom with a gun. It was my father's old pump action .22-caliber rifle. I was given great responsibility and freedom with it since I grew up on a farm with few people around. I had just finished using it. The gun was full of rounds and I was unloading it over my bed. Instead of unloading it properly, I was unloading it as if I were firing it quickly. Holding the gun at a slight angle over the bed, every shell entered the chamber and ejected with the complete action as I pumped the handle back and forth. This process was okay until I got the skin between my thumb and index finger caught in the action of the hammer. Startled and hurt, I pulled back, which pulled the hammer back just enough to come down on the pin and fire that round. The explosion of the birdshot round in the gun went into the wall, just on the other side of my bed.

I was horrified! I went from being super cool one minute to being outside my body the next. My brain wasn't working right, my heart rate was out of control, and there was a fear sensation in my body I didn't understand. I was freaked out. I knew my mother and father were in the next room as I stared at the hole, wondering how I was going to fix this mess in a few seconds. My mind quickly thought of how much trouble I was going to be in. My heart was pounding out of my chest when the door flew open and my mother and father rushed into the room. They thought I had shot myself. I remember the panic on their faces, and I remember how badly I felt about it. I broke down emotionally, not even knowing why I was crying. They were so relieved to see I was okay that we never even discussed the hole in the wall. They could tell I'd suffered enough.

I wish I could have shown my son that the damage to our room didn't matter. I wish I could have held him and told him I forgave him.

I don't know whether what I have described is what really happened with Canyon or not. Until now, I've kept it to myself, except to share with my family.

The coroner's report says that my son killed himself. He did, and the question, "Why?" will always trouble me.

# The Unquenchable Question

*"Trust your instinct to the end
though you can render no reason."*

~ Ralph Waldo Emerson

Why? What a haunting question "Why?" can be—especially when it has no apparent answer. The residue of questioning left after seeking answers to the impossible encumbers the soul. Although the questions have been there and have created strong emotions at times, I've learned, at least in this case, that it's fruitless to pursue them. Why did my son do this? Why did he put the gun to his head and pull the trigger? The question is powerful, but I have no way of answering it. No one knows but Canyon. The question is important and at the same time, unimportant. The answer could heal, but it could also be destructive. The question, "Why?" needs to be answered, and yet it doesn't. Sometimes that question whispers to me, and at other times, it screams.

Our minds are conditioned and built to seek for answers and a sense of closure. Why would he kill himself? This question brings up so many others, leaving me with a constant churning of doubt and self-degrading thoughts. Was there something I didn't know? Was it my fault in any way? Did I do something to cause him to take his life? All these questions and more happen in a brief second. Some of them linger and continue to haunt. Especially the personal questions, such as, "What did I have to do with this? What portion of it was my fault?" I'd left a gun in an unlocked closet in my room. That was clearly something I controlled. I had grown up around guns and so had my children. I had taught them to treat guns carefully and with respect. Yet, it was too trusting and stupid of me to assume none of my children would ever handle a gun without my permission.

But why would Canyon have been so scared or worried about the consequences of whatever troubled him that ending his own life seemed like an option—even in a moment of extreme emotional confusion? Why? I don't know. I know that earlier in the day his mother and I had been upset with him over not getting some yard work done. It didn't seem like a big deal, but I'll never know whether he had perhaps taken it harder than we knew. Were we too hard on him? Did that play some part in his emotional turmoil after the first shot? Did he contemplate how disappointed we might be with him, again?

Canyon was absent-minded by nature, so it may have seemed to him like his life was full of constant reminders about what he had forgotten to get done, or what he hadn't done right. He was a sweet and loving person. He was always sensitive towards others' feelings, perhaps because he was a

# The Unquenchable Question

sensitive person who felt both love and hurt more deeply than others did.

Writing this book brings up issues I've rarely felt comfortable enough to discuss with anyone. When the topic comes up in conversation and someone asks how Canyon died, I usually say I lost my son in an accident. If they ask what kind of an accident, I respond, "A gun accident." They seldom ask another question about why, and I don't feel I owe any more of an explanation than that. Calling it an "accident" gives my family, my son, and me the dignity of not focusing on "suicide." I suppose it doesn't really matter what I call it. We live in a world that condemns suicide, and understandably so. I believe no person has the right to take human life, whether the life of another or his own. Many others feel the same way, which contributes to the uncomfortable sadness and sense of taboo around suicide.

Yet, I believe we should talk about it. I believe more people should talk about it. My son and I never had a single discussion about suicide. Why? I guess I never felt the need. I guess I thought he valued life the way I did. I don't know what it feels like to consider seriously taking my own life. However, it has been researched and documented that as many as ten percent of people, at some point in their lives, have had thoughts of ending their lives, or have had thoughts of it being an option for them.

I never had the discussion with Canyon that I would love him no matter what, and that though I might be disappointed in his actions at times, I would always love him. Why didn't I have that discussion? I guess I always thought my general actions and words showed it. I guess I thought he knew. But if he had really known, wouldn't he still be here today? That question will haunt me like a residue from his death that I may never clean off. However, my mistakes from yesterday cannot be my mistakes for tomorrow.

The reality is that, if I choose to, I could create an inquisition and bring all the guilty parties to trial in my own mind. I could easily cast myself as the father with unreasonable expectations for how his kids should be. I could set up my own trial for all who may have some blame in Canyon's death, including Canyon and lash out at all of them for letting this happen. I believe blame is one of the major obstacles marriages face after the premature loss of a child. One parent or both blame him- or herself or the other to the extent that one can never fully forgive or trust the other again. The shame or guilt can cause a depression where people can't be present for themselves, let alone their spouses.

This questioning has never completely gone left me, not even after eight years. I don't know whether it ever will. I feel healthier when I don't spend too much time dwelling on the questions, except for those honest ones such as, "How can I do better now?" Some may need deeper answers to these questions. They may need a fuller sense of closure. They may feel a need to identify an exact culprit or reason. I don't believe there's any right or wrong in having such needs for closure; however, many questions can never be answered. Sometimes we just have to submit and make a choice to move forward in faith, and be conscious of what we decide to focus our attention on.

There are many things I don't know and will never know

about my son's death. But there are some things I do know. They are positive things. They are things so large and grand that in spite of all the unanswered questions, they carry me forward with faith, courage, and hope. These are the things upon which I've learned to focus. They are the gems I must treasure. They are the opportunities for me to be a better person, a better husband, a better father, a better son, and a better friend. They are the things worth sharing.

# GRIEVING

# PREMONITIONS

*"Every adversity, every failure, and every heartache carries with it the seed of an equivalent or greater benefit."*

~ Napoleon Hill

While Canyon's death was completely unexpected and almost surreal, I do feel Cologne and I got some small hints, some little premonitions that perhaps Canyon's time on earth was not meant to last long. There were certain times when Cologne especially had a sense of his mortality, an indescribable feeling of just knowing.

As a toddler, shortly before I met him and Cologne, Canyon had a near death experience. One day while playing in the yard, he squeezed, unnoticed, under a pool gate. His uncle, who was mowing the lawn, had a strange feeling come over him that he should look in the pool. He found Canyon face down, floating in the pool, and rushed to save him. From all signs and appearances, Canyon was dead. Fortunately, they were able to revive him. Cologne recalls her son gave a strange account of the event from his perspective. In his little toddler voice, Canyon told them that after he fell in the pool, he floated up over his body and saw himself in the pool. Then he went and got his uncle and told him to go get him out of the pool. Perhaps the strangest part is that his uncle concurred that, although he didn't hear an actual voice, he did feel as if someone was telling him to go to the pool.

Canyon was very book-smart, but everyone who knew him agreed that he was a bit like Curious George when it came to "common sense." He was full of curiosity and wonder, but he didn't always have the good judgment to keep out of trouble. Canyon was normally a responsible, obedient child, but due to his absentmindedness, he had brushes with death throughout his life. Upon several occasions, he could have easily gotten seriously hurt or even killed. Cologne recalls having felt a certain premonition that he wasn't meant to live long on this earth.

The night Canyon died, right before we left on our date, a brief wave of fear washed over Cologne and left her with the distinct impression that one of her children would die that night. Although Cologne has always been a protective mother, she describes that particular impression as being something different from her usual motherly sixth sense. It shook her up enough that she ran about the house, nervously making sure the baby gate was up over the stairs and that everything was in order before we left. She then did what most of us would do and brushed off her feeling as nothing more than an odd thought that didn't need to be taken seriously.

# Premonitions

In retrospect, Cologne doesn't think she felt that premonition in order to change the future, but rather, to be a bit more emotionally prepared for it. One huge blessing for her has been that even though it hurt so much, she feels in her heart that perhaps it was Canyon's time to go, and in some strange, cosmic way that we can't explain, accidents aren't always accidents. They look like accidents—random, pointless, and unnecessary—yet in some hidden way they are the very opposite. Things happen for a reason, even if that reason is completely hidden.

I believe there is truly a grander scheme for our lives. Beyond the tragedy, the heartbreak, and the disappointments, there is, somehow, a pattern and a purpose behind it all. Many parents have experienced the heartbreak of losing a child. It is not my intent in any way to diminish their loss, nor my own, but I will say I firmly believe that ultimately, everything will be okay—somehow. Perhaps not now, and perhaps not for a long time, but as someone who believes there is more to our existence than just this short mortal life, I do believe the day will come when everyone will understand their losses. We'll understand why they happened and why it couldn't be another way. On that day, not only will broken hearts completely heal, but even the deepest scars will disappear.

Even though he's not here with me in a physical body, at this moment I know that Canyon is okay. He is happy wherever he is. I don't need to mourn for him; I need only mourn for myself and for my loved ones who miss him deeply. Yet, no one lives forever. One by one, some sooner than later, each one of us will go where Canyon is, and then we'll truly understand that he is all right. All of our loved ones who go before us are all right. They are all alright. We don't need to worry about them. They are in the hands of a loving God. For me it has made all the difference to trust in God, to trust there is a grand plan, and to believe that not one of us needs to waste our life worrying about the what-ifs and the what-could-have-beens. Instead, we need to invest passion in the precious moments we do have because life is fragile.

I've learned to recognize that though my losses hurt, and I may not understand them, there may be dormant in them the seed of some great benefit that, with watering, nurturing, and patience, may be realized later. Although I know this now, it was nearly impossible to see when I was sitting in the heat of the fire.

# ROLLER COASTER OF EMOTIONS

*"No one ever told me
that grief felt so like fear."*

~ C.S. Lewis

NEGATIVE EMOTIONS ARE NOT "BAD." In my opinion, they are good because they give each of us the opportunity to savor the sweetness of positive experiences and emotions. How would we know we were happy if we didn't know how it felt to be sad? And yet our negative feelings can become destructive if we unconsciously choose to hang out with them like bad friends or onto them and let them control our actions from behind the scenes, like the man behind the curtain in *The Wizard of Oz*.

After Canyon died, I found myself busy with caring for my family, which made it difficult to think of much else. The opportunity to feel a full spectrum of emotions like anger, sadness, fear, and guilt moved aside for the time being as I cared for their needs. Yet as we moved forward and tried to get back to normal, I started to feel those emotions well up inside me like a volcano getting ready to erupt. Sometimes that internal "volcano" expressed itself differently.

At times, it felt like an explosion where a lot of destruction occurs instantly, and other times it seemed like a gradual flow of molten hot lava that burns and destroys slowly. Each emotion was different and each one came like a nighttime invader to obliterate my peace.

## ANGER

The first strong emotion I had to work through was anger. It wasn't immediate and, fortunately for me, it didn't last long, but it was there, and it was real, like a sledgehammer pounding away at the door of my soul trying to destroy something precious inside.

My feelings of anger resulted in my not communicating with my family. It resulted in my being more selfish and self-centered regarding what I wanted as opposed to what was good for the family. I was short-tempered, quick to resent, and had little patience or tolerance for much of anything.

Fortunately, I was able to recognize it. I didn't dwell on it and understood my son's mistake was just that—a mistake. I knew in my heart that in his right mind, he never would have shot himself. He never would have hurt his mother and father in this way, and he never would have hurt his brothers and sisters the way he did. He certainly wouldn't have intentionally created a situation that would traumatize his younger brother and sister and potentially encumber their emotional development. Canyon was a loving person. Whatever decision he made, it wasn't to hurt anyone else.

Still, anger scratched at my soul with its intense need to blame and resent. It pounded on the door trying to get in. I do not doubt that if I had fully let my anger in, the destruction it could have wrought would have left parts of my life in irreparable ruins. Still, I definitely felt the strong allure of anger. It would have been so easy to be angry. It would have been easy to be angry at not only the situation, but at anyone involved, especially at Canyon for the "careless, selfish way he had left his family." That was one thought I had. That it was cruel of him to leave us this way.

I was only truly angry, however, with one person—me. In my need to assign blame, I found myself the easiest target. I was angry because I didn't have that old rifle locked in a safe. I was angry because I had just assumed it was fine to have a gun unlocked and sitting in the closet. I had grown up in an environment with that kind of thinking, so it seemed natural to me. We didn't have a safe when I was a kid, and I didn't deem it important.

Canyon had been around guns, and I'd taught him to follow safety protocols and handle them with respect. Yes, I'd heard other people talking about how important it always is to lock up your guns. Had I really thought they were making too much out of it? How ignorant I was to ignore good advice, and I hated myself for my cavalier shortsightedness and carelessness. How could I ever forgive myself for this mistake? I couldn't help but wonder whether Canyon had made a split-second decision in a moment of confusion or weakness that never would have happened if the gun hadn't been accessible.

I was angry at my own stupidity and lack of forethought. Anger is a vicious emotion. It cankers the soul and steals energy from the body, leaving one void of power and lacking the ability to be inspired and productive.

# SADNESS

Once I began to let go of anger, the snarled blanket of sadness slid over me like a black cloud of soot that held me tight. It wouldn't let me breathe. I felt as if it were robbing oxygen from me, and I would suffocate, just like I had felt the night Canyon died. Other times, it left me paralyzed and helpless. Most of the time when I was trying to perform my daily duties, I felt that if anyone were to blow on me or look at me strangely, I would break down crying. I felt this way at work many times. When I worked with clients, I sometimes felt uncomfortable and exposed, as if they could see it in my face or written on a sign on my forehead. Before Canyon's death, I had never felt such deep sadness in my life, and at times, I literally thought I was going to die, or that I was slowly dying inside.

My children, bless their sweet and precious hearts, wanted to do simple things with me, but I just didn't have the ability. I felt helpless and tired. I'd never been able to relate to people who had depression until then. Now I felt as if the world had left me stranded and alone. I was just sad. Looking around, I had no real reason to feel as badly as I did; at least, that was what I told myself. Plenty of evidence said I still had an amazing life before me, and I still had much to be thankful for. I still had a marvelous home and a wonderful family that loved me. I still had good health, caring friends, and physical comforts.

All the evidence seemed to suggest we would be okay and survive this experience somehow. But, nonetheless, I was just sad. It seemed at times that I would never be able to do anything about it. I'd get over it for a short while when I chose to engage myself in some activity that captured my attention. But then, that damn blanket of sadness would catch up with me and follow me around until I was completely enveloped and trapped again.

# FEAR

As the cloud of sadness started to dissipate, an unknown emotion appeared that was just as crippling as what I'd already experienced. Fear. I'm not one to fear much, but I've always battled with fearing what other people will think of me. Now I felt completely exposed and vulnerable.

It was as if the cloud of sadness left me naked and exposed to the world with nowhere to hide. I had countless questions I was afraid to ask, much less try to find their answers. What would my friends think of me? Would they wonder why my son shot himself? Would they wonder whether Canyon had some kind of problem? Would they wonder whether I was a bad father?

How could I face the world? Would people know I felt like

crying all the time? Would they know I felt lost and alone? Would they know I felt helpless? Would they think I was a fool for not having the gun locked in a safe? Would they not want to be my friend because of what had happened? Would they respect someone whose son shot himself? Would they always wonder? Would their unanswered questions trouble them just enough so they couldn't be comfortable around me? Would they ask questions I couldn't answer? I didn't have any answers. I just wished people wouldn't ask questions. I was tired of talking about it and not having answers.

What about my work associates and clients? What would they think of me now? If they had thought I was a "good" person before, did they think I was "bad" now? Maybe I wasn't a good person. Maybe I was "No Good." Maybe I would never be any good again. How would I support my family? Would I ever get back to my normal self? My best friend didn't come to see me... why? Did he think less of me now? Did everyone think less of me now? How will my children live with this? What's going to become of them? How will they deal with all the questions curious friends and careless strangers will ask? Is this going to overburden their lives? Will it ruin their lives? Will my wife survive this tragedy? Will we ever be the same again? Will our marriage survive? How can our marriage survive this loss?

All these questions and many more raced through my head on a constant basis, and at times, seemed to seize me up. How could I go on? Each step seemed to come with some sort of trepidation about what was around the next corner.

# GUILT

Guilt was the next emotion. What role had I played in Canyon's death? Why was this tragedy part of my life? What could I have done differently? Guilt was the worst of all the invading emotions; it kept sleep from my eyes, incapacitated me, and eroded my life and self-esteem. It tore at my soul and forced me to deal with questions I shouldn't have had to deal with. It made me question who I was and wonder whether I was good enough to be my children's father. At times, the thought stole into my mind, *Would they all be better off without me?* I truly wondered whether they would be better off with me gone. Should I give up my role as a father and husband because I didn't deserve to be one? Doubt after doubt rolled through my mind like haunting ghosts, stealing ambition from my soul.

Everything, every little thing I had ever done wrong in life rushed into my mind and caused me to question my very being. Although I thought I had been a good father and husband for the most part, and though much evidence seemed to support that truth, I still questioned everything.

I really knew I had done the best I could. I knew it. But for other lingering questions, no clear answer existed. Knowing that I could have locked up the gun made everything worse because that was clearly something I'd had control over. Because I felt blame for what had happened, it made the questioning that took place in my mind a very dangerous gauntlet to run.

Guilt is the one negative emotion that can always haunt my soul if I choose to let it. It's the one negative emotion that, for me, is the hardest to get rid of because it is the one that requires me to forgive myself.

May Canyon's mother forgive me. May my children forgive me. May the rest of Canyon's family forgive me. May Canyon's friends forgive me. May Canyon forgive me. But can I ever fully forgive myself?

I have no sure or easy answers for how to overcome guilt or sorrow. I question many things and even find myself resenting some of the things I have been told. The one thing that seemed constant was people would tell me, "Time heals," or "Time will make it better," or "Don't worry; the pain will go away in time." Hearing such statements quickly became annoying to me. "How do they really know?" I'd ask myself. "I'm sure it goes away with time, but only because we become used to it. We become numb, but is that the same thing as 'going away'?"

My resentment of people's parrotted comments increased. I knew they meant well, but I had no faith in their words because most of them had no idea, no real experience with the grief I felt. I look back now and realize how much people cared, how genuine they were, and how hard it must have been for them to say anything at all to me and my family. I love them for trying now that I have the opportunity to look back from a different space than the space that hurt so badly. Somehow, I convinced myself at the time that no one knew my sorrow. Surely, no one could understand the deep gut-wrenching sorrow that stole all breath and made me feel like I was suffocating. Surely, I would die of heartache, if not, from the sheer burning pain of suffocation.

# RUNNING ON EMPTY

*"Courage is not the absence of fear,
but rather the judgment
that something else
is more important than fear."*

~ Ambrose Redmoon

---

I can't seem to get anything done at work. I start my day and work through its dance, and at the end of the day, I'm ready to pick up my keys and head for home. I look at the yellow legal pad that started the day with me. It has a long list of things. At the top of the list are the well-known words "To Do," and the page is full.

I browse over the list and realize I haven't completed even one of the items. Almost every task that I started the day with the intention of doing is still on the list; only a few have lines through them. I place the list back on my desk and head for home. I'm physically and mentally drained.

Things are different for me with Canyon gone. I'm not the same person. The drive home seems like it's three times longer, and I find myself getting emotional as I'm trapped alone with myself in my car, waiting for traffic. I don't know why I feel so emotional, but I do.

I arrive home and greet my wife and children, but not very well. I go into my bedroom, and as I stand at the foot of the bed, I loosen my tie and take it off. I unbutton my shirt, which seems dreadfully difficult. Why do these easy tasks seem to be exhausting? I allow myself to fall face first onto the bed and I don't get up. My entire body aches, especially behind my eyes. They burn a little and feel like they want to throb out of my head.

Am I sick? Why do I feel this way? As I lie there, I don't want to move. I haven't had dinner, but I don't seem to care. I pretend to be asleep when my daughter comes in to say, "Hi, Daddy." I don't move or respond. I don't have the energy to get off the bed and finish changing my clothes. I wonder whether anyone will care if I fall asleep like this.

I wake, it seems like moments later, to my wife nudging me and saying I should get up, get changed, and get under the covers. I look at the clock; it's nighttime, after eleven o'clock. I'd arrived home five hours earlier. With a guilty feeling, I get up, remove my clothes, climb back into my warm bed, and fall asleep again.

---

This pattern repeats itself, but the troubling part that continually haunts me is the yellow legal pad with my "To Do" list that just keeps getting longer. I'm not able to be productive during my workday; that frightens me. If I don't figure out what's going on soon, my family will be in financial danger.

I returned to work two months after losing Canyon. I was amazed to see my absence hadn't affected much. People were patient, and they helped where they could while I was gone. But now it's different. I've been back to work for a couple of months now. My clients are dependent on my performance and they expect me to get things done. My income is one hundred percent based on commission, so I am at risk of not making any money for a while, and I am concerned about my sales pipeline. I seem to be busy during the day, but at day's end, I realize I have been scattered and unable to focus. The biggest mystery to me is why I am tired all the time. I need to figure something out, fast.

One day I get home from work, crash on the bed, and sleep all night, still wearing my work clothes. When I wake up, I still don't have the energy or desire to do anything. I don't want to go to the office. I decide to call in sick. But I'm not sick. I am just exhausted. I wonder whether I have mono or chronic fatigue syndrome. Not knowing what to do, yet instinctively knowing I have a problem and must be sick, I decide to go to the doctor.

He asks whether there have been any big changes in my life recently, and I tell him about losing my son. He leaves the room, comes back in with a clipboard and pen, and asks me to answer a series of questions. Then he leaves me to answer his questionnaire. The questions seem to revolve around depression. Some questions ask whether I've ever felt like taking my life. I've never experienced anything like that or recognized within myself any of the symptoms of depression.

I finish the questionnaire as he returns, takes the clipboard, questionnaire, and pen, and leaves. He's gone for some time. When he returns, he sits down next to me. He tells me the questions I've just answered are a way to determine a person's level of depression. I don't hear everything, instead I hear, "You have failed the test miserably." He says, considering all I have been through over the last four months, I am suffering from a form of post-traumatic stress disorder. He's sympathetic and compassionate. He tells me he's impressed I've done as well as I have. He tells me not to be concerned—it's pretty normal under these circumstances. He encourages me and says, "Don't be hard on yourself." Next, he tells me he thinks he can help, if I'm willing. I agree.

He scribbles on a prescription slip, tears it off the note pad, and hands it to me as if he believes it's the answer to all that ails me. The prescription slip says something I can't read. He explains the prescription is for a small dose of an antidepressant. He explains what it is and how to take it. "It will take about thirty days to get into your system and start working consistently," he says. "But I think it will help a lot."

I feel awkward and give him a look of disappointment, not for what he has done, but because I feel disappointment in myself. There's an awkward pause before he says, "It's up to you to decide whether you want to take it or not, but I'm pretty sure it will help. Once you feel like you're back to your old self again, you'll be able to stop taking it."

I thank him and walk out to my car. I sit in the car for a few minutes before starting the engine. My emotions are a little uncertain. In some way, the feeling of relief is overwhelming, and I feel like crying. I feel discouraged to have an antidepressant prescription in my hand, but relieved at the same time to know a reason exists for the way I feel, and that there's a possible solution.

---

Months after losing my son, I had been on call around the clock for my wife and children. I'd frequently been up late into the night comforting different members of my family for anything from sleeplessness to nightmares, and during the daytime I'd help deal with their feelings of confusion and grief. I hadn't taken very good care of myself during this time because I'd been concerned about everyone else. I had not really taken any time for myself. We received help from so many people, but there was just so much to attend to, so much to take care of and worry about. Physically, I'd gone as far as I could go on my own, and I could go no further. My body had been telling me to slow down. Now it was time for me to decide to swallow any pride I might have had concerning my ability or inability, and move on the best I could with help.

My feelings of inadequacy would not get in the way of my decision, and I wouldn't let my feelings cripple me. I was determined not to let my family suffer because of my pride. That would be too big a price. I felt relieved for having had the courage to seek help, and now that I had a name for what had been happening to me, I had hope that there might be a solution. I swallowed my pride, and I swallowed the pill, literally and figuratively.

This time was very fragile for me, and I was on the verge of tears most of the time. I felt like someone could blow me over with the slightest breath or look. It took all I had to stand up and go into a business meeting. I had always been courageous about my life and business, but it took everything I had just to get up in the morning, let alone handle any difficult business discussions. I just had to lean into it and trust that everything would work out. I did, and as the doctor promised, the medicine started to take the edge off after about thirty days. I was on my way again.

For me, the medicine was a lifesaver. I am not pro drugs. I am one of the last people who believe the solution to life's challenges comes in a pill. Still, I can't deny that the medication gave me a greater ability to function at a difficult time in life. I continued to take it for about four months. When I felt I was sufficiently back in the flow, and I found passion again for what I was doing, I stopped taking it.

Our performance in life is generally based on our ability to face our fears. Psychologists have determined our fear of public humiliation is even greater than our fear of death. I was afraid to meet with people after losing my son. I was afraid I wouldn't be able to perform the way people expected me to. I was afraid I would humiliate myself in front of a client or co-worker. I was afraid of what people might think of me because my son shot himself. I was terrified to fail in front of my peers. I had been courageous in the past and had spent years overcoming fears, but then, just like that, I was full of fear again. Fear growled in my ears like a grizzly bear standing over me, ready to tear me from limb to limb.

Most people, if asked, would probably say they were not aware I had suffered so greatly. They knew it was a sensitive time, but they probably had no idea it was as hard as it was. But that which we persist at, we get better at. When we do something difficult, we gain additional information our brains don't fully comprehend at the moment. It goes deep into our cells and becomes a part of our neurology. The next time a similar situation comes up, even though we may not consciously be aware of it, we are able to respond according to what we've learned from expanding our horizons. For that reason, I feel faith and courage are immensely important to the grieving process.

As a society, we tend to be afraid to cry. We're especially afraid to cry in front of others. Yet giving myself permission to cry at an appropriate time might make me more capable of not crying at a time that may not be appropriate. Our bodies seem to learn as they progress through experience. Every subsequent trial makes us stronger, and the courage becomes a part of our physiology. The difficult part is to find the courage and to survive the first few times.

The courage to live graciously during and after a loss is a huge challenge when you lose a loved one. For some, it may be their greatest challenge. I imagine for the elderly person who loses a spouse, the courage to go on living is very difficult at times. Our courage gives others permission to be courageous too. Just as men at the edge of a battlefield draw strength from the courage of their leader and those around them, each of us can give courage to others. I've found when others see me coping with my challenges in life and living well, it gives them permission to do the same with their own challenges and fears.

One of the unexpected effects of losing Canyon was that I started writing. I'd never really considered myself a "writer." Yet, after losing my boy, many of the barriers I'd built around myself throughout my life seemed to wash away with my tears. I stopped focusing on what I was "supposed to be" and how I was "supposed to behave." I think the less self-conscious I became, the more willing I was to express myself. Writing was a safe, cathartic way to process my feelings and emotions. Occasionally, I found myself writing short stories, poems, or just random thoughts as I waded through the confusing emotions that swirled thickly around me. One poem helped me to verbalize and identify the confusing fear and the battle of grief that was raging within me.

## BATTLE OF GRIEF

I stand on the edge of a great battlefield,
Before me, a mighty army: Doubt and Fear.
I tremble at the thought of the battle before me.
Have I been here before?
The fear of death screams in my ear.
My body trembles, tempted to turn and run.
Yet my heart stands firm in its resolve,
Willing to submit, but why?
Could my body turn and leave my heart behind?
What would happen then?
I'd be unable to face another battle without my heart.
So I judge this battle more important than my fear.
Please heart, keep my body near.

~ Sean M. Fleming

# SLEEPLESS NIGHT

*"In our sleep,*
*pain which cannot forget*
*falls drop by drop upon the heart,*
*until in our own despair, against our will, comes wisdom*
*through the awful grace of God."*

~ Aeschylus

I DON'T PRESUME TO KNOW HOW THE MEMBERS of my family survived the aftermath of Canyon's death. Each journey has been a uniquely personal experience. I even hesitate to share their experiences because I realize I only saw the surface of them. I may never know what took place in their hearts and minds.

Cologne, as Canyon's mother, suffered terribly in ways I cannot even begin adequately to understand or describe. I only know how her reaction affected me personally and how her journey influenced mine. At times, Cologne's suffering seemed to be all-consuming. I ached for Canyon. I was acutely aware that our family had suffered an unspeakable loss. Things would never be the same. Yet, I desperately wanted my family to continue forward, to focus on the many good things still in front of us.

On some levels, my healing process progressed more simply than my wife's process. I don't mention this fact with any pride or guilt. Over the many months of trying to fix the mess our lives had become, over the many months of my feeble attempts to comfort Cologne, I came to the realization that I could not fix anything that had happened. I couldn't fix anyone. I could not take away her pain. I couldn't even comfort her unless she would allow me to do so. Sharing her pain with her didn't lessen it. My becoming wrapped up in her despair as I tried to help only seemed to make matters worse. It was as if I were being pulled under the water by someone who was drowning. I couldn't save her. All I could do was physically be there until she resurfaced from the pain that washed relentlessly over her. I could only throw her the lifeline. She had to choose whether to grab it.

Sometimes, as Cologne agonized over Canyon, all I could do to stay sane in my helplessness was to put my thoughts to paper. I wrote whatever came to my mind, right or wrong. A nameless mix of emotions ranging from fear, to love and resentment, fought for space on the paper in front of me. The following paragraphs are some of those entries, written five years after losing Canyon.

# Sleepless Night

I sit here wondering, amazed at the confusion we create in our minds as to what is real and what is false. At the moment, I am happy, content, and quite peaceful with my life in general. By most people's standards, I am quite blessed. I find comfort in the love and beauty around me. I have my health. I am reasonably intelligent. I am able to enjoy life on a level that allows me to look forward to tomorrow. Today was nice, in fact, and I recognize success in the little notes of progress. I'm at peace and able to be still and contemplate the gratitude in my heart. I'm content with being here now and will create my next moment, but that is not a thought as much as it is momentum. This is genuinely how I feel at this moment and most of my time is spent in this same state of mind. "I'm grateful for life" is the short list, and the long list would fill this page, and many others, with gratitude.

My dear wife, on the other hand, is quite haunted at the present moment and her heart is full of sorrow. She currently lies in bed on the other side of the room, fighting demons in her mind. I can't help her; she won't let me. It's not that she won't let me. She can't. She doesn't know what to do. It renders her helpless and alone. She feels abandoned, and yet she has so much around her. Everyone wants to include her, but she refuses to see it. I ask her how I can help and try to cheer her up, but she tells me, "It's okay." She says I don't need to cheer her up, and she'll be all right. I walk away and sit down after I tell her I love her. She breaks into a wail that sounds like a wounded animal that is alone and sick in the dark. I hate the sound; it frightens and repulses me. It sends chills down my spine. I cry for her and wonder why it is like this. Why does she need to go through this much pain? How much is real and how much is created in her mind? Even that which may be created is real to her, and therefore, I cannot tell her to calm down. I cannot tell her to look at the incredible things about her life. I can only let her be and hurt for her as she cries out in pain. I don't want the children to hear her crying. It's an unsettling sound, like someone in extreme pain, but not sudden pain. It's a pain that won't go away, a prolonged pain. It is the sound of anguish, a deep sore unhealed. It sounds like the crying of a soul in bitter darkness, lost and alone with no options. It's the sound of despair and hopelessness. There are many options all around her, but she is in a prison inside herself.

I've been through this many times. It's becoming second nature to me. This is why I'm writing right now, as I'm hurting for her. I used to let this process play its toxic battle on me. I was so involved in trying to pick her up from this state, to help her pick up the pieces, but at times, she turned her anguish toward me. Now I realize the unfruitful nature of that process. It actually served to create a sad, co-dependent relationship. I needed to make her better, and she needed me to give her the extra care I gave when she got this way. Not anymore.

I love her, but I can't give any more of my soul to the black hole. Since this realization, I've been able to be there more often for her and the children when it really matters, not just for these outbursts of emotion that erupt like a sleeping volcano that's abruptly awakened to cover everything in smoldering ash.

# Sleepless Night

The crying has stopped now and I hear a soft sigh that remains uncomforted but seems to realize that I'm okay, so she can be okay. I don't really know what's right and what's wrong. It's confusing. I hurt for her, but there is nothing I can do. So far, the best thing I have found is to do nothing. Sometimes that hurts even more. I don't think she has any idea of the damage her hurt is doing to the rest of the family and the people around her. I know she doesn't mean to hurt us. She is innocent in that respect. It hardly seems fair that she has to go through this type of darkness. Sometimes it gets so dark that I've questioned whether she would be here the next day. She has even said when she cries, "I wish I could die," or "I feel like I'm going to die." I cannot compare this feeling with anything I know. I'm helpless to understand her feelings because they are foreign to me. I wish I could take away her pain. I wish I could help.

Tomorrow she'll be fine, and everyone who knew things were not okay today will be confused and walking on eggshells. We move on in this confusion. Why? Because we love her. She is my wife. She is my children's mother. Though crippled and helpless sometimes, she is still the one we love. Though she may lash out at us at times, she is still the one we love. Confusion? Yes, but what can we do? What do we do?

---

Life certainly didn't always go this way, but when it did, it was dark. The only thing I could do was be patient. The only thing I could do was not judge. I cannot claim any talent in either of these attributes. What could I do? I didn't adequately know or comprehend at the time. I struggled with how to help her when I hardly knew how to help myself.

# SORROW COMES IN WAVES

I BELIEVE WE NEED TO ALLOW OTHERS TO BE WITH US in our grief. However, while I could have benefited by allowing others to be there for me, at other times, it was good to be by myself without the distractions of those who wanted to help. There were times when I didn't want to see another soul and just wanted, needed, to be by myself or with my children. I believe this need is normal and healthy in moderation. I found tremendous value in the times when nobody was around, and it was just me, by myself, or I was just with my wife or children so we could talk to and encourage each other. We spent a lot of time talking about Canyon and all of the unique and quirky things he did. We laughed and we cried, and as we did, our hearts filled with wonderful experiences and memories of him. One of us would remember something about Canyon and someone else would add to it.

We all had collective experiences with Canyon, and precious moments that were unique to each individual. Hearing these stories shared added to our bank of memories. We found great value in these moments and frequently sought them out as a family. One of the greatest benefits to this activity was the incredible awareness it created for each of us to recognize the impact he had made in each of our lives. I also believe that as we shared these memories together, the emotion attached to them helped sear them into our memories, each at a different level, but each time to a greater extent than before.

At times when we were together after he died, we were sure he was with us, enjoying our spirit, while we enjoyed his. I believe those moments were a benefit to him, and as time passed, I came to a greater understanding of how, when I was in a state of sorrow and grief, it was actually harder for me to be close to him. When I was suffering, my memories were not as clear, and my appreciation and gratitude were encumbered. When I was calm, I could recognize the incredible treasure he was, so I felt closer to him. I believe he was closer to me then as well.

This understanding leads me to discuss something I still struggle with: The issue of those who cannot overcome their pain and sorrow after losing a loved one. Although I completely understand this pain, I've learned that people do themselves (and those around them) a disservice when they prolong their suffering and sorrow by dwelling on the loss and pain.

Life is meant to be celebrated. Even if you don't believe life goes on after death, you can still recognize life is precious and celebrate the tiny moment of life you had with your loved one. If you do believe that life goes on in some form or another, as

I do, why feel sorry because someone has journeyed to new heights of existence?

I learned wonderful things about my boy after he passed on that I might not have ever learned, or at least appreciated the same way, while he was alive. I certainly don't mean my life is better this way, but losing Canyon taught me to appreciate my other children on a different level. This awareness only came from having the presence of mind to celebrate his life and the value of his life. I learned to see little gems, such as the red-shell sand on the beach in Hawaii.

Canyon paid a tremendous price so his family and others who knew him could have an added depth in their lives, a new way of seeing the world that we couldn't have experienced in any other way. This experience is impossible to put a price on and shouldn't be compared. I honor my son best when I live in a manner that would make him proud of me as a father and a man.

We have all heard stories about parents who, after losing a child, withdrew from the rest of the family, either out of guilt or sorrow. The result is not a loss of only one person, but instead, of many. A father, mother, or another sibling is also lost in the withdrawal. How tragic to lose a loved one who is physically still around, but has emotionally disconnected.

Momentarily, my own children lost their mother and father as a result of our loss. They've certainly encountered other types of suffering based on their parents' moods and emotions. Because I hurt so badly and struggled to do things Canyon and I had once done together, Kevin suffered for a while by not being able to do things with his father. Kevin shouldn't have had to pay this price, but I couldn't do much about it at the time because I was lost in my own sorrow.

My sweet wife's capacity to be a mother was also diminished at times because her mind was so encumbered by grief that she just couldn't cope. Depression was dark and, as a result, there were times when there wasn't much light, fun, or nurturing to give. Our children, bless their hearts, learned to step up and take care of themselves and each other, and they learned to have deeper compassion for others.

I believe everything happens for a reason and sometimes that belief helps. All I can do is give it my best. I enjoy as much as I can about this process, and I try not to judge any of us too harshly along the journey.

I think sorrow is critical to overcoming grief. Sorrow is honest. It is real and raw. It allows us to go deeper into our feelings and beliefs. It allows us to be in a state where, hopefully, we can accept help from others. Sorrow heals and fills the heart with real truth—the kind that can never be denied. All of us must grieve, and it is critical that our grief be complete or it will keep returning in unhealthy ways.

Sorrow comes in waves, and just as with waves in the ocean, the more you fight it, the more tired you get. But if you submit and work with sorrow's waves, you can eventually learn to surf them. The more we are able to accept sorrow and submit to it, in an appropriate way, without a fight, the better sorrow will serve us. I still have times when out of the blue I get a thought that causes me to feel like I need either to smile or cry about Canyon.

The smiles are greater these days than the moments when I could cry at any time. But it still feels good to cry once in a while and let out the energy of emotion that builds up inside.

# Sorrow Comes in Waves

At times I have just been driving down the road when I have found myself overcome with feelings of sorrow and sadness. At times, I have been in meetings during the workday when I didn't know whether I could do any more work because I felt weak and drained. Other times, I would go home and just crash, or I would not be able to be there for anyone—including myself. Learning how to grieve and move forward has been a long process for me.

# GRIEVING

I'll never know whether I have grieved well or properly. I have only my experience and my perspective. I do know, however, that if I were to go back and do it again, I'd do some things differently.

If you were to ask me how I would advise people going through the grief of a loss, I'd begin by letting them know we're all different—as each loss is different. We are all on a different schedule. Be kind to yourself and know there is no right or wrong way. The important thing is that you get back to the unencumbered you, and sooner rather than later.

To begin, decide that you want to find a way to move beyond where you are. Be honest about how you feel and get all of the emotions and feelings out—don't hold anything back. That said, not holding back is not something we all do well. It's certainly not something I've done well over the years. Oh no, I've been good at just the opposite. I've kept those feelings to myself and shoved them even deeper when necessary so no one could see me in such pain.

During the long weeks after Canyon's death, my emotions were sometimes so strong I didn't know what to do with them. I had to shove them down, so even I wouldn't have to deal with them. In my opinion, some of this behavior was a self-defense or self-preservation mechanism. I believe the subconscious mind goes through this process to protect us until we're strong enough (if ever) to deal with terrible trauma. The mind puts "No Trespassing" signs around events and issues of a trauma to shield us from what is too painful to endure in that moment. At some point after the shock of the trauma or loss has passed, the mental "No Trespassing" signs come down, allowing those protected emotions to emerge. Sometimes, they don't come down for years, and not without good counseling and help.

There are many ways to lower these barriers of suppressed feelings which show up as negative emotions and limiting decisions in our lives. The process starts with giving ourselves permission to be vulnerable, honest, and to experience the them as they occur rather than pushing them back down. Do whatever it takes to experience the full swelling of emotions, and don't worry or fear what others might think.

Writing can be a great way to start. After you get the energy moving, it's easier to be more expressive vocally. Don't hold back. Go to a quiet private space and yell or get loud about it. Hit a pillow or talk to a chair. Imagine someone in that chair, then talk, yell, cry—tell the person how you

## GRIEVING

feel. When you feel safe, talk to someone you trust and love. Seek help from a counselor or spiritual leader. Talk it out. I believe the more we talk about things, the healthier we become. Talking with others gives us a different perspective than what we are working with on our own.

I'm speaking from experience when I say that life can be very lonely if you have suppressed emotions, especially negative ones such as anger, sadness, fear, guilt, or shame.

If I could go back and do something differently, I would have spent more time talking with my family about my feelings and the importance of sharing emotions. Not just for myself, but for them also. I would have done even more than I did to give my family a safe place to process their emotions. I think if you ask anyone who knew us at the time whether we did a good job of processing our emotions, they would probably say yes. What I did not do very well, however, was trust my wife and children with seeing my emotions all the time. For the most part, I kept them to myself. While my family was able to experience and express their own emotions around me, I didn't feel safe enough to let them see me express my feelings. I think it would have been better for all of us if I had openly expressed my feelings because it would have given them permission to do the same.

Instead, I processed most of my emotions on my own, either through writing, while long distance running, or on long drives. This solitary processing was helpful and I needed to do it. It certainly helped me.

We don't get a redo, as nice as that would be at times. We do get to move forward with new insight and wisdom. We can improve as we go forward, helping ourselves and others along the way.

What I've learned in retrospect from this experience is that the best grieving I've done has been when it all comes gushing out like a flash flood full of debris and forgotten pieces from other tragedies and pains I've collected over the years. In the past, I have avoided this kind of emotion. I grew up believing it was some kind of weakness I had to hide.

"Don't cry now; people will see and know you are weak," was the thought that ran through my head. But those held-back emotions build up like water behind a dam. I've kept them back somewhat, but all kinds of leaks allow the emotions to get out in both high-pressure streams and little drips. The debris from all of those prior traumas, losses, tragedies, pains, mistakes, sorrows, and regrets pummel the dam and weaken it. When I open the floodgates, so to speak, and allow myself to be honest and let the real emotions flow forth, then I release the pressure from all of that built-up energy. We stop up that energy when we refuse to let it flow, but it needs to flow freely if we are to be healthy. We need to release that energy in order to learn to deal with it. The benefit of just letting it out is that it will actually help you to be less emotional at inappropriate times.

My resistance to letting it flow held back a lot of untapped energy that could have been very useful in my journey. Expressing my grief did not come easily to me, and most of us were not taught to grieve very well. Culturally, many of us are taught that emotions are a weakness, and we should even ignore some feelings—at least the kinds of feelings that cause us to be honest with our vulnerabilities.

# Grieving

I look at the power of a river and relate it to the life force that flows through me. If we allow a river to flow freely over time, it can carve a great gorge through rock and earth.

It is the same with man. If we allow our life experiences to flow through us, rather than stopping them up behind an emotional dam, they can shape us. If we acknowledge our feelings and nurture them, we can realize value from every experience. Our emotions can be very powerful and create greatness.

The experiences in my life build who I am, and they give me character, awareness, and a capacity for strength that is forged through my journey. If shared, these new strengths can benefit others and nurture and enrich their souls too. We have all been through experiences that give us the opportunity to be who we dream, or dreamed, ourselves to be.

We tend to think experiences such as the loss of a loved one or other losses are setbacks because they hurt, tear us down, or slow us down. Some of us even let these experiences beat us down for too long, even permanently. For me to think I am going to get through life without having to endure the pain of losing a loved one is very naïve. It's egotistical and self-centered to believe life always ought to be easy and painfree. There's no way that is going to happen. I'd like it to be that way, as I'm sure everyone would, but the reality is that we will all face tragedies that will shape us. We will all face adversity. We must do so in order to grow.

I know I have a choice. I can let my sorrows beat me down, or I can live my life the best I can. There really doesn't seem to be any other option for me. What does it mean to live my life the best I can? What type of life do I imagine? These are questions only I can answer for myself. I think I hold back too much. I think most of us are shy with our abilities and true feelings; at least, I know I have been. I wonder what each of us could do, and contribute to this world, if we were truly open to our feelings. If we harnessed that power and honestly let it flow through us, not constantly forcing it to dam up and stop us, what would life be like then?

That river of emotion is constantly changing. Sometimes, it is a powerhouse of hydraulics capable of changing the earth's shape. Other times, it is a trickle in a dry riverbed, trying to find its way through the rocks and boulders in its way. Either form is fine, and each one has its purpose. Even a trickle of water can nurture life and soothe a cool or weary soul. Just let it be, let it flow, and recognize what it is, when it is. When it's the high-volume earth-changing flow, then I have the choice of channeling it and changing my world for the better, creating energy and power along the way, shaping my future and nurturing other thirsty souls. But if undirected and out of control, it has the power to destroy everything in its path.

When it is the slow trickle, I have the choice of feeling bad, weak, and sorry for myself, or patiently waiting for nurturing, filling rains to come. The rains will eventually come, in due season. In the meantime, the trickle can still be there and might even be able to soothe a weary soul who might also be lost in the desert of life. Each type of emotion has an opportunity for good and bad, and each of us has some power to direct that flow. Either way, tremendous power exists in just noticing and acknowledging how you are feeling emotionally and being at peace with it.

# THE VOID

*"What is the worth of a soul?"*

~ Paul C. Child

Within weeks of losing Canyon, as we sat at the dinner table, I looked at my family. I was happy to be with them and their distinctly different personalities. Their desire to tell me about what happened in each one of their days filled my heart. However, something was wrong; it felt like half of my family was missing. The table was so full and yet so empty. Only one was gone, but it felt like there was a greater void. I looked each one in the face. Everyone was there, all except for my son Canyon, yet, my family felt so small without him.

I was and remain grateful for every one of them and acknowledge how much each one contributes to my joy as a husband and father. I am proud of them for how they dealt with the emotional trials they have had to endure. Still, it was difficult for me to get over the emptiness I felt. It's amazing how important one person can be to a group. When the individual was a critical component, and then is no longer there, those left behind begin to look for ways to fill that void. Conversations are different and people feel loss in ways they don't consciously understand. The worth of a soul is immeasurable, and the void that is left is difficult to explain. I don't love any one of my children any more than the other. I cherish them all completely. This void, however, was a massive cavern I couldn't understand. It tore at my soul and would not leave me alone. It haunted me at times. I didn't know how to deal with it.

My wife, four children, and I sat at the table, a pretty good-sized family by anyone's standard, yet for years after Canyon's death, whenever we were together, I had moments when I would look around and think, "Where is the rest of my family?" I never spoke to anyone about my feeling that someone was missing from the table, and I tried to act as if I were just looking around casually.

The kids frequently asked, "What's wrong, Dad?" and I'd reply with something along the lines of, "Everything is fine. We're all here together, and I'm just enjoying myself with all of you." Truly, I was, and yet I constantly had that haunting feeling—the void I could do nothing about.

One time at Disneyland, I actually went into a brief panic. I didn't know what I was missing, but the feeling that surged through my body was adrenaline-laced. "One of my children is gone!" was the thought that rushed through me. It was silly because if Canyon had wandered off at Disneyland, I wouldn't have worried so much about him as about one of my younger children because of his age. Yet my heart skipped, my breath got short, and I was full throttle in a panic. Then, just like that, I realized what I'd felt, but I

# The Void

was troubled. It affected me as if one of my little ones had disappeared. I felt silly and confused. Cologne understood exactly what had happened to me and helped me brush it off.

It still occurs sometimes, although I've become much better at allowing it to be just a passing thought, a gentle reminder of how important he is to our family. Each person is a critical piece in the meaningful puzzle we call family.

I've learned to recognize that particular feeling as an opportunity to acknowledge my children for the incredible people they are. I compliment them for being such a critical component of who we are as a family, and how much we would miss them if we ever lost one of them. I try to take the opportunity to let them know how important they are in ways that didn't come so naturally before.

Each of my children had to deal with this void in a different way. They unknowingly would do things to fill the void. When there is a vacuum, something will fill the space, and it can be filled with good or bad. The stir of both positive and negative emotions makes it easy to fill the vacuum with negative behavior and emotion. At times, our children vied for attention, both from their parents and others, often because since Canyon's death, they weren't getting the kind of attention they were accustomed to getting. Looking back, it's a miracle we all emotionally survived the chaos.

Another void we've had to deal with is the space left in a conversation when it comes to the subject of my son. Often when I met someone new, the person would innocently enough ask, "How many children do you have?" My wife and I gave different answers to this question at different times. To whom did we owe an explanation? And to whom should we not talk about Canyon's death? We both knew the correct answer was five, but a space of time passes when you evaluate what to say, wondering whether it will perhaps need an explanation later, and that seems to create a pause. Often I'm not in the frame of mind to say anything about it. It seems like a very simple thing, but the complexity of who, what, and when to tell was often a burden. It sometimes put me in situations I would have rather avoided, or it could be too much of a burden on the person to whom I was talking. It was such a big part of our lives. We lived with the aftermath twenty-four hours a day, seven days a week, but it seemed a potentially awkward and painful issue to dump on someone merely making a polite inquiry about our family. Who, when, and what to tell became a social study, and one that was better left to that inner voice—that little feeling of when you should, or shouldn't, do something. This burden was practiced with many ungraceful attempts, and sometimes the void of silence in a conversation seemed eternal.

I realize the people I had these conversations with may not have recognized the void as I did because they were still processing the gravity of what I had just said, but to me, it sometimes seemed to go on forever. That dreaded awkward pause was a deafening silence. There was even a time when I thought that if I had to tell one more person what had happened, I just might implode into myself, never to recover. Those days went on for some time and were accompanied with many awkward moments of choked up conversation and wet eyes. Although at times I despised

# The Void

these moments, in retrospect, they might have been good for others, because of the way some would open up to me after. Eventually I got better at handling these moments more gracefully and naturally, if only by gradual experience and conditioning.

# THE MERIT OF DISTRACTION

*"Grief fills the room up of my absent child,*

*lies in his bed,*

*walks up and down with me,*

*puts on his pretty looks,*

*repeats his words."*

~ William Shakespeare

I HAVE NO CLAIM TO GREAT ADVICE FOR ANYONE facing "The Void." You ache to fill that emptiness with something, anything, and everything after a loved one leaves you. Again, something will fill that void. Whether consciously or not, your mind will seek out ways to fill this void—sometimes with good things, people, and activities, and sometimes with destructive things, people, and activities.

For this reason, I believe tremendous value exists in intentionally distracting yourself at times with good things that focus your energy on the positive aspects of life. It can be wise to limit intentionally your opportunity to dwell on the negative feelings of loss. I don't advocate burying your pain or denying it, but rather respectfully acknowledging it's there and still choosing to live your life. Distraction is different than avoidance. Total avoidance of pain can be a dangerous trap in and of itself. It can cause you to shut out the pain or deal with it in an inappropriate way.

At times, I found myself feeling guilty for not spending more time thinking about my son and the memories I have of him, but at the same time, I realized there was some merit to keeping myself distracted when the pain was raw. Sierra was a tremendous value to me in dealing with the loss of Canyon. Sierra was only five-and-a-half months old when we lost him. My last memory of Canyon is of him holding Sierra close and saying goodbye to us in a playful voice (as if he were Sierra) as Cologne and I left for our date. He held her up and helped her to say goodbye to us with a wave of her little hand. She was so innocent and delightful and served as a valuable distraction as I focused my time on her and her needs. The same was true for the rest of my family.

Sierra became the focal point who drew attention when we needed it. When someone started to get sucked into negative behavior because of the loss, Sierra would require our attention; focusing on her needs helped us to feel better. She must have known things were somehow different, even as an infant, but inherently, she knew how to live in joy and peace. She taught us to live and breathe again. She hugged and cuddled us when we needed to be hugged and cuddled. When we just didn't have the capacity to offer it on our own, she nudged her way in and freely gave the love we needed.

Sierra was our little angel who, by just being herself, helped fill the void in a big way. Someone else, like a child, a sibling, or a parent in need, might fill the void caused by the

# The Merit of Distraction

loss of a loved one with other pursuits, such as participating with us in a new hobby or activity, perhaps with other members of the family, which could strengthen a sense of connection between parents and children and between siblings. Will a pottery class or taking up kayaking dissolve your pain and make everything okay? No, of course not. But it might distract you from the pain long enough to rest emotionally, so you have the strength to carry on another day.

# MARRIAGE AFTER DEATH

*"Nature gives all, without reservation, and loses nothing;
man, grasping all, loses everything."*

~ James Allen

Eventually, if we don't constructively fill the void left by a child's death, it can easily fill with conflict. Many marriages do not survive the death of a child, especially a tragic death such as suicide, where it is too easy to assign blame and see each other as nothing more than a reminder of how things went horribly wrong. However, many marriages do survive, and even thrive, after the death of a child. Statistically speaking, only sixteen percent of couples who experience the death of a child get divorced. According to studies by the parental grief support group, The Compassionate Friends, less than half of those divorced reported the death of their child as a factor in the decision to divorce.

Yet, there is no doubt that the death of a child will strain a marriage. Couples can pull through the devastation and make the marriage even stronger over time. The initial havoc created by a child's death is hard to understand until you've experienced it. My relationship with my wife suffered tremendously. The loss somehow creates an emotional environment where it's easier to focus on all the other little problems that were never addressed, perhaps because nothing was there to magnify them—just as a magnifying glass might magnify warts on the back of a hand.

My wife suffered greatly, and although I understood the loss, I could never fully understand the relentless pain she went through. She had undergone the pain of labor and giving birth after carrying Canyon for nine months as he developed inside her. He was her first born. She felt guilty that perhaps there was something she could, or should, have done differently. She took on the blame in ways that made little sense to me, ways I thought she had no right or reason to take on.

We had some very dark times in our home that most people will never fully comprehend. At times, the despair was so thick it was almost smothering, and I was afraid to let people know how bad it really was. I was able to help at times; other times, I just wanted to give up. But because giving up was never truly an option for me, sometimes that stubbornness actually made it worse.

I look back and wonder what I could have done differently. I'm not sure I have any answers, and I don't want to pretend that I do. Everyone's situation is different. I believe I hindered my wife's progress through this process because I was afraid to be myself. I was afraid of how it might threaten her, and how she might feel left behind.

# Marriage After Death

She resented how I seemed to be doing so well at times, and she even accused me of not loving Canyon enough. "Don't you miss him?" was a common question when she was in pain. It was as if she resented me for not crying as much, or as often as she did, as if her way of grieving was the only right way to prove how much we loved and missed Canyon.

There were times when I would have taken all that pain from her and born it myself if I could.

I found, however, that my lessons are not necessarily for others, but for me. There is a time and a season for everything and everyone, and until someone is ready, that person will not have the same experience I might hope they will have. One of the biggest points of frustration was how we felt we should live our lives in the wake of our loss. My opinions and hers were quite different at times, even spanning opposing ends of the spectrum. The passion each of us had in regards to his or her own way was often intense. It became difficult (sometimes impossible) to compromise.

For example, I thought we should celebrate Canyon's life on the anniversary of his death by doing something he loved and enjoying time as a family, as if he were there with us. It's what I thought he would want us to do. She, however, thought nostalgia would help her feel better. I interpreted that to mean she wanted to hang out in a dimly-lit room and contemplate his death by doing things like reading the notes we got from his friends and classmates or going over photos of his life and crying for hours.

Neither one of us was right or wrong. We just needed to mourn and move on in two completely different ways.

I wanted to focus on the active lifestyle and fun we had experienced with Canyon and keep our minds off any negative thoughts of his death. Her need was to mourn and read all the great things people said about him in letters. Crying seemed to be more healing for her. She thought it would be the same for the children and me. I felt the last thing I needed was another cry. I thought if I lost any more water to crying, I might dry up and blow away. Then what good would I be to anyone?

I wanted to keep the family distracted because I feared going back into mourning again. It had been such a painfully dark time. I didn't want to go back there after finally breaking through to some light. I don't know if my resistance was more for my family or myself. There must have been some of both, but I felt no good would come from all of us sitting home and crying any longer. Canyon wouldn't want us to do that, I thought. He would want us to have a good time and remember the happy times we had shared with him. Because of how differently Cologne and I viewed things in this respect—and although we didn't know it at the time, because we lacked the communication skills to get through it—there just didn't seem to be any graceful way to have this discussion.

Our children were caught in the middle. From my perspective, they wanted to empathize with their mother, but they weren't eager to go into mourning again either. She couldn't see it my way, and I couldn't see it hers. It was a difficult thing to compromise on. So she did her thing, and I did mine. The children were, consequently, required to choose sides at times. It only served to separate us more.

## Marriage After Death

Most of the time, the kids chose to go with me because they didn't want to cry anymore, either. Cologne then just felt worse, like we were abandoning her. It was not until six years after Canyon's death that we didn't mope through the eighth day of December again. I imagine it will always be a difficult time of year for all of us. I've learned from "experts," and from my own experience, that even if a certain practice or ritual seems therapeutic and healing to one spouse, it might have the exact opposite effect on the other spouse, causing more separation, misunderstanding, and sadness. Grieving differently and being unable to accept or understand each other's grief was one of the major obstacles in our marriage as we struggled to recover from the death of our son.

Even though I didn't grieve the same way Cologne chose to grieve, I can't deny that tears can be healing. I have to make a real effort not to cry at times. So sometimes I don't try. I just cry. I imagine there will always be times when both of us cry about losing our boy. Crying reminds me that I'm alive. The most precious times are when I'm lying in bed when nobody else is around—when my thoughts go to Canyon and I recall something about him that brings a smile to my face. Those smiles are generally followed by a few teardrops when my eyes well up so much that the fluid cascades over the corners of my eyelids and down the side of my face, sliding into my ear or dripping onto my pillow. I've learned not to hold those tears back because they often lead to comforting thoughts.

But it was a challenge to grieve with someone else. Some nights, there was a void between the two of us when we crawled into our bed, when we both hurt so much and didn't know how to console each other. We each needed someone else to make the effort, but most of the time, neither one of us was able. We'd both lie there in bed hurting, with a space between us that felt like an impenetrable force field.

It doesn't feel safe to go into that space. It's a danger zone. You don't know whether you have the strength to go there, and if you do and are rejected, you may not come out emotionally whole. It's a dark space nobody wants to talk about, and the longer it stays there without being breached by one or the other, the thicker and more destructive it becomes. That void is usually filled with harsh words a couple of days later. I dreaded this space and feared it.

At first, I avoided this space like the plague, until I realized how destructive avoiding it was. Once I learned that, I figured out how to fill this void, even when I thought I had no strength left. At times, Cologne also was able to fill the void and come in my direction. Such magic should always exist in a marriage. When one can't, the other makes up the difference. Yet the reality is that it's very difficult when two people are hurting so badly. They both think they need someone to fill the empty void for them.

Constantly trying to fill this void can backfire. Often I ventured in to console when I thought I had nothing left in me to give. I tried to love her in ways I recognized were lacking in me, instead of in her, and I began to resent it more and more until it became an obligation I was performing out of duty rather than love or compassion. I unknowingly created a different kind of danger zone that made a difficult situation even more fragile.

It's difficult to give more of yourself when you think you have given so much and feel depleted of energy and love. This empty feeling was sometimes masked by many different feelings, but when it came down to it—it just didn't feel safe. It was easy to stop sharing, to grow apart.

I found it easier to give when I remembered Canyon's giving personality. I remember him giving his mother a kiss, or handing her a wilted bouquet of dandelions, or presenting her with something he'd made for her. He would do anything for his mother to show her how much he loved her. That's what children do. They don't hold back their love; it's unconditional. He taught me so much with his ability to forgive and forget my faults. I asked myself, "What's the worst that can happen to me if I live by the example he set?"

I think of the smile he brought to his mother's face when he said, "I love you, Mommy," or "Can I hold you, Mommy?" And I asked myself, "What prevents me from doing the same in a completely unconditional way? What prevents me from seeing what she needs?" Although there may be things about her pain and sorrow that I might not fully understand, I do appreciate her love for him and her loss. Oh, how I appreciate her loss. But beyond the loss, I see our little boy smiling at me, offering me a lesson in gratitude and unconditional love, teaching me the best way to love his mother.

# CAN I CHANGE THE STARS?

*"Suffering is universal;*

*how we react to suffering is individual."*

~ Robert D. Hales

One might say that the art of living well is really the art of letting go with grace. Life is loss. We lose jobs. We lose lovers. Some of us lose children. And some of us even lose ourselves. In the lonely aftermath of loss, it's easy to lose sight of the beauty we are mourning. Like a child who's been crying for so long that he eventually forgets why he's crying, we lose sight of what we're missing. We stay focused only on the void left behind. Like staring at the spaces between the stars, rather than on the stars themselves, we see only darkness and let the lovely lumens twinkle in vain.

We can learn so much from sorrow. It is a master teacher to those who are open to the journey of tears. These tears can truly turn to tears of joy, a joy no one can take from you and no loss will diminish. This joy will help your light shine brighter.

Choosing to let my light shine, even if dim at times, is the only choice I can make. If I let life's suffering knock me down, who benefits? If I live my life the best I can, in time the pain will subside, I will get better, and, through a ripple effect, those around me may benefit as well. Like throwing a pebble into a pool of water, the waves ripple out to create what is around it.

How I choose to think of and focus on my son—his death or his life—and the energy I put into it becomes my experience. I can focus on the loss, or I can focus on the light of his life. Where does the ripple effect stop if I choose to live by focusing solely on the loss—would it ever stop? Similarly, by living my life celebrating and sharing the light of his life, how great could the ripple effect of good become?

The tragic loss of Canyon will continue to change lives because of the way those who knew him choose to live based upon the lessons they learned from him. I must freely allow his light and mine to shine forth and not dim it in any way. I have an opportunity to live, love, and give, and in the process transform myself; by my example, I give others permission to do the same.

I am fully aware that life's journey will continue to be difficult at times. But I am slowly learning that life's adversities are what refine us and actually make our light shine brighter. One of the most brilliant materials known to man is the precious metal known as silver; when polished, silver has a mirror finish in which we can see ourselves. However, before silver can shine so brightly, it must go through an intense process.

# THE SILVER APPRENTICE

Many years ago when a young man wanted to learn a trade, he would put himself in the care and instruction of a master and become an apprentice. He would completely submit to the master's care and hope to learn enough that one day he would be good at that trade so he could provide for himself and his family and contribute to society.

One day, such an apprentice was before his master from whom he had spent years learning the trade of refining silver. Now his training was nearing an end. He had learned the trade well, and his master was proud of him. Over several years, the apprentice had learned all the steps of taking raw ore and refining it to the most brilliant precious metal known to man. In the process, he had also learned about refining gold. Now he was ready to start his own business of refining precious metals.

His master asked him, "Of all of the things you have learned under my care these many years, what would you say is the most valuable thing?"

The apprentice paused as he thought of all the things he had learned under his master's care. This man had taught him so much, and he was now fully prepared to go out and be a refiner on his own. He searched his mind and his soul. One thing stood out, but he wasn't sure whether it was what his master would want to hear.

"Well, sir, you taught me well. You taught me to find good ore. That task is not easy; it takes knowledge and hard work. You taught me the correct way to mine the ore, which is very difficult and dangerous work. You taught me how to crush the ore, which is backbreaking work that never seems to end, but you taught me to do it well and make it fine, which is very critical. You taught me how to prepare the slurry for the furnace, which must be done with precision and care under the heat of the sun. You taught me how to heat the furnace and get it to just the right temperature because the heat of the furnace is the refiner. You taught me how to fire the material and to be patient in the process of separating the dross from the precious metals. You taught me so many skills to get a final product that is pure and desirable. They are written down and in my head, and they are great in number. However, there is one thing that I learned under your care that I believe is more important than all the silver in the land. But I'm not sure it's what you wish to hear because it really has nothing to do with refining silver, sir."

"What is it?" asked the master. "What is it you have learned from me that is more important than all the silver in the land?"

"Sir, for many years now I have labored and learned under your care. You taught me much about our trade. I was not always grateful; many times I wanted to quit and run away from the hard work and the pain of the labor. It was very trying at times. Often I doubted what I was doing and whether I was of any worth to you or anyone. I'd ask myself, "Is what I am doing worthwhile?" One hot afternoon, soon after I had started in your care, I was crushing ore; the sweat from my brow was burning my eyes and I could hardly see. I wanted to quit and go home, but you said something to me that stuck with me.

"You said, 'Young man, there will be times in life when you want to quit, to give up and walk away from your trials; in the moment this happens, pause, and sit in the fire of your affliction a little longer; good will manifest, but only as you submit to your lessons and are willing to endure the fires of adversity.'

"Sir, each time I saw you polish the silver after we finished the process, and it shined that brilliant glow, I remembered the dirty, dull ore our silver came from. I remembered how it had to be located, pulverized, and put through an intricate refining process with intense heat and patience. Was it not a refining process I went through myself to learn what you have taught me? Are we not all like the silver? You taught me that only by sitting in the fire of adversity can a precious element be separated and brought to its purest and most brilliant state."

The master was silent, with a satisfied look in his eyes. He may have taught the apprentice how to refine silver and gold, but the apprentice had taught himself to submit to his own journey and be transformed by his own furnace of adversities.

After a moment of thought, the master looked at the apprentice and said simply, but with great satisfaction, "You have learned well. You are prepared now to be your own master."

An ancient Chinese proverb says, "Pure gold fears no fire." It doesn't fear fire because it cannot be destroyed by the fire. As eternal beings, we cannot be destroyed by the fire of adversity, but as natural men, many times in life we want to turn and run from our trials. The heat from the furnace of our afflictions and trials seem as if it will burn or even destroy us, so our instinct is to "get out" and we want to turn and run. However, if we pause and endure the heat of the furnace a little longer, we may find that the heat is actually refining us and transforming who we are, giving us the ability to handle new trials with a little more grace. By doing so, our light will shine a little brighter. By doing so, we can be more consciously aware of how we are being refined by these trials and how, what we do, affects others.

Everything we do in life—all our choices and all our actions—has a ripple effect in some way. Seemingly little, insignificant things like the way I greet my children each morning might help make the start of their day just that much better. The ripple effect that transmits into the environment around us affects those around us in meaningful ways.

How we choose to handle our trials, the choices we make, and even our thoughts ripple out into the environment, because ultimately, the way we think affects our actions and the choices we make, therefore, creating how we live and our future.

If we are wise, like the silver apprentice, we will recognize that to refine ourselves, our actions, our words, our choices so we produce not only silver but gold in our lives, we must first learn to submit to the lessons that come from our trials.

# HEALING

# THE RIPPLES OF A FUMBLE

*"When one door of happiness closes, another opens,
but often we look so long at the closed door
that we do not see the one that has been opened for us."*

~ Helen Keller

FOR KEVIN, LOSING HIS OLDER BROTHER led to frustrations at school. For one thing, he had been a top student, but after Canyon's death, Kevin's grades suffered, and he struggled to get them back up. He and I have had many conversations about how his brother's death affected him. On one occasion, a family friend asked him how Canyon's death had changed things. Kevin opened up a bit and shared, "Before Canyon passed away, I liked to talk. Now my family has to pry things out of my mouth. I don't know how to speak anymore. The hardest part is that my family feels loved when people communicate with them. But I can't talk anymore, so they feel like I don't love them. I try to show them that I care, but I feel like I can't. I live in fear I'll disappoint somebody that I love." Kevin has since described himself as feeling like his voice was lost or taken from him.

After you've lost someone you love, little bits and pieces of everything else can get lost as well. This situation was certainly true for Kevin. Some of his memories of what took place the night Canyon died, and how life was before his death, are starkly different than my own. Seantay remembers, or doesn't remember, things differently than the rest of us too. That's okay. I learned that not only is this normal, but there's really no way around it.

When our family went to grief counseling, one thing the counselors said stuck with me. They said our children's remembrances and views about what had happened would likely evolve and change as they grow older and their understanding of life deepens. They were correct; I've discovered that each individual experiences grief and loss differently. All of us lived through the same event, but we all experienced it from our own unique perspectives. Kevin internalized the events of that dark night in a way that makes him feel like he's "lost his voice." This reminds me of that recurring dream I used to have when I couldn't shout out a warning or cry for help.

Some of Kevin's hurt turned into resentment toward me. He resents me for being hard on Canyon for his forgetfulness, which, at times, frustrated his mother and me. He wonders whether Canyon might still be alive if I'd been a more patient and understanding father. I wonder that too.

I know I wasn't perfect. I was just a father, trying to do my best. As a father, I did some things very well, and in other areas, I just stumbled along as I tried to raise my family. When Canyon ended his own life, it left all of us with unanswered questions.

# The Ripples of a Fumble

I know Kevin loves me. I know he wants to be close to me. We both want that. I desperately want him to forgive me for any blame he may have assigned me in regards to Canyon's death, whether deserved or not. Yet his anger and resentment toward me for not preventing his brother's death became a confusing wedge between us. I believe that over time Kevin will come to understand the situation differently, perhaps when he becomes a father himself. Perhaps one day after a disagreement with his own teenage son, he'll realize that fatherhood doesn't come with a manual, and that we're all just fumbling along doing the best we can with the knowledge and understanding we've been graced with, which at times seems woefully limited.

I already know I've made mistakes. I already know I wasn't a perfect father and never will be. I wasn't a perfect father to Canyon, and I'm not a perfect father to Kevin or his siblings. But no matter what, I've always tried to do what I thought was right. I believe Kevin will come to recognize that, and it will allow him to let go of some of his frustration, fear, or resentment toward me. It will allow him to forgive.

I can't imagine what it was like for Kevin or Seantay to find their older brother that night in a pool of blood. It was a horror no child should ever have to experience, yet it happened. I can't make it go away. I can't bring Canyon back, and I can't heal Kevin's wounds or take away what he saw. But I can try to understand his anguish. I can be patient with him and wait for the day when he feels safe enough to be close to me again.

# MOMENTS OF REGRET

*"Until you make the unconscious conscious,
it will direct your life and you will call it fate."*

~ Carl Jung

Although I firmly believe in forgiveness, including forgiving myself, I don't think it's realistic to say we shouldn't have regrets. We all have regrets of one kind or another, but that's all right, as long as we don't let our regrets consume us. I believe we can acknowledge that we wish we had done things differently, while still forgiving ourselves. As the saying goes, hindsight is 20-20. I know I and my family were doing the best we knew how at the time, trying to make it through life, just like everyone else.

Once, in a moment of frustration, I was so unusually harsh on Canyon for not respecting his mother that I struck him. The experience is difficult to share, but at the same time, I feel compelled to share it because I believe it had a lasting impact on all of us. I share it to illustrate that we don't get to choose how our actions will affect others. To leave out this part of the story solely to spare myself from embarrassment and shame wouldn't be right. The lesson here is profound for anyone ready to learn. The regretful moment left its mark, and I can pretend it never happened, or I can learn from and share it.

When Canyon was fourteen, Cologne had frequently asked me to do something about him not listening to or respecting her. I didn't recognize his actions as reflecting a lack of respect so I wasn't sure how she wanted me to deal with the situation. I don't think she really felt that way, either, but rather she used those words in an effort to feel heard and validated. As parents, dealing with a teenager was uncharted territory for us since Canyon was our oldest, and we were certainly not experts; all we had to go on was how we were raised ourselves and what others had told us.

The next time I noticed Canyon saying something disrespectful to his mother, I overreacted. Clearly, he shouldn't have said it, but it didn't warrant my reaction. I struck him on the left side of his head with my open hand, knocking him across the kitchen floor. He was only fourteen at the time so he was easily overpowered by his father. When he rose, I struck him again. I got no reaction from him until the fourth time when he realized it probably wasn't a good idea to get up again. He just sat there on the floor, crying and looking up at me, waiting to see what I would do next. My anger faded and turned to guilt as I noticed the hurt, confused look on his face. I knew I had made a serious mistake. I had failed him and my family by losing my temper. For a moment, I thought my actions would show him just how serious it was not to respect his

# Moments of Regret

mother. I thought I had to teach him a lesson. But what I had done was wrong, and I knew it. To make it worse, the looks of horror on Kevin and Seantay's faces pierced deep into my soul. This wasn't the father they knew.

Canyon and I both learned a lesson that day, but it wasn't the one I'd intended. I learned that something that happens in a flash of emotion can cause endless regret. I learned that you don't discipline in anger, and I vowed never to strike my children again, a vow I have kept to this day. I was sorry, very sorry, and I asked for his forgiveness. Being the kindhearted person he was, Canyon offered me forgiveness quickly and wholeheartedly when I admitted my mistake. I tried to find the ability to forgive myself as well.

I will always regret my behavior that day. I don't regret that it hurt him physically as much as I regret the emotional damage it did. It shook him up and created emotional scars. Emotional scars may be invisible, but they are worse than physical ones. I regret hurting his tender trust. I regret giving him reason to doubt—or even to fear—me.

He didn't know what he'd done wrong when I unleashed that violence, and I'm sure he wondered why I was defending his mother so inconsistently. I regret that my other children saw it because it scarred them too. I regret that I took out my frustration on Canyon, frustration that was really directed at my inability to communicate better with his mother about her frustration with him—maybe she wouldn't have been so frustrated with him if she had felt better heard by me.

When he was young, Canyon was especially sensitive to the feelings of others, a trait he carried into his teenage years. He seemed to have no biases toward others and didn't hold grudges. People noticed and liked him for his ability to accept all people for whom they were as well as their potential, without focusing on their faults. He was incredibly loyal as a son, brother, and friend. Even so, I believe my poor response left its mark on Canyon and the entire family, especially my son Kevin, who was only seven at the time.

Later, about the time Kevin turned fifteen, he slowly started to withdraw from me. He went from always wanting to do things with me to finding all kinds of excuses not to. At times, he would become silent when I tried to hold him accountable for his actions. It was difficult for both of us. He seemed unreasonably scared when I felt I hadn't given him any reason to be afraid of me. It was frustrating because he wasn't communicating with me. I didn't handle it well because I was constantly questioning him, which caused him to shut down and resist me even more.

Eventually, I understood this distancing was rooted in our past, so I tried to give him the space to be honest and authentic with me about his feelings. One day, in a tender moment of exchange when he could finally open up and share with me, I learned that when I had to remind him of his responsibilities, or I appeared disappointed with him in any way, he felt confused and scared. My actions triggered in him a fear that if he disappointed me, he'd somehow end up like his brother. This fear was a tremendous burden for a young man to carry and not completely understand.

When I realized the pressure I was creating for my son, I started to cry. I'd never struck Kevin, but he'd come to believe my frustration and Canyon's death were linked somehow. He thought maybe Canyon would still be alive if his father hadn't made him feel like a disappointment earlier that day. Kevin needed months to overcome this negative trigger once we discovered it. It took a tremendous amount of patience and work as a father to regain Kevin's trust, and I'm still working to earn it back.

# HISTORY REPEATS ITSELF

We all experience moments that shape our lives. For better or worse, these changes form our universal viewpoint and color our perspectives. They create a blueprint that governs or triggers our actions and responses. I believe my outburst in the kitchen those many years ago may have affected my young children, especially Kevin, more than any of us knew at the time, becoming one of those life-shaping experiences. When I was much younger than Kevin was at that time, I lost a bit of trust in a parent too, without being consciously aware of it, and it affected me deeply for much of my life. The older I get, the more I realize how, through words and actions, each generation influences the next, in both obvious and invisible ways. Like riding a merry-go-round, we find ourselves circling back to the same place from where we started, usually without even realizing it, as history repeats itself over and over again, until we choose to break the cycle.

I hesitate to share this publicly. I want to protect my mother's memory in every way. I worry it may be disrespectful to share her one serious mistake, when the truth is that in almost every way she was an extraordinarily wonderful mother. She loved and cared for my siblings and me with all her heart. I forgive her for being imperfect, just as I pray that my children forgive me. However, I feel that this particular incident that I am about to share was a part of my journey, a part of the "ripples" that start in one life and end up radiating into others' lives as well. Each of our lives (including yours, mine, and Canyon's) is effected generationally. These ripples are not to be mourned or obsessed over, but to be recognized and forgiven.

When I was a young parent, my mother asked whether I had ever forgiven her. At first, I didn't know what she was talking about. I assured her I had no ill feelings toward her and had completely forgiven her for anything she might be holding onto. She quietly said she really didn't understand how I could have ever forgiven her.

"Forgive you for what?" I asked.

"You don't remember?" she replied.

"Mom," I told her, "you've been an incredible mother. I only remember you showing kindness toward me."

When she started crying, I could tell this burden had been on her mind for a long time. Her heart was aching. She had been carrying a secret guilt and pain over something terrible she had done to me many years before. I could tell how she felt, but I still didn't know specifically what she was talking about. The more I tried to think of something, the more confused I became about why we were even having this discussion.

However, I could tell she felt it was her moment to come clean and ask for my forgiveness, something she needed to express for her own healing. I put my arms around her as she began to tremble and sob. I felt strange and guilty for not remembering something she seemed to think was so important.

"You don't remember the time when you were little and I lost my temper with you?" she asked. "It had nothing to do with you, but I took out my anger on you—for something your father had done... You wouldn't listen to me, and so I struck you over and over. I picked you up and threw you on the bed. Over and over I struck you and picked you up and threw you back on the bed again."

She shared the whole experience with me. She was sobbing uncontrollably. I felt a flood of emotions rush into my body as she struggled to regain her composure.

"You kept saying, 'It's alright, Mommy. I won't do it again. It's alright, Mommy. I love you. It's okay, Mommy, please don't hurt me.'"

She continued to cry as the painful memory seemed to envelop her. I felt very awkward. I put my arms around her and explained again that I must have forgiven her a long time ago because I didn't remember. The mother I had always remembered was kind, compassionate, and very gentle. She had taught me how to love and appreciate life. She had never intentionally hurt me.

"I've spent many years trying to make amends for how I hurt you that day. I've thought I would never be forgiven. You were only three years old. You didn't know any better. I wasn't mad at you that day as much as I was mad at your father and took my anger out on you."

My head hurt. We were both emotional from the

heaviness of the conversation and painful memories. I held her tight and repeated that I had surely forgiven her, and I would forgive her still. She only whimpered sadly in response. I encouraged her to lay down on the couch and rest. She quickly fell asleep, exhausted from the emotions.

Years later, through a series of events and my own emotional healing, I realized that my mother had been referring to an event that had caused a part of me to shut down emotionally and to reserve my trust. What happened had damaged a part of me emotionally, so I decided I wasn't going to risk getting hurt again. As a child, I blocked it out so it was easy to forgive my mother. I had put a "No Trespassing" sign around my memories of that experience to protect myself, without being consciously aware of it. Yes, children are good at forgiving, but the decision I made as a young child had long-term consequences because once installed, a "No Trespassing" sign is difficult to take down.

My mother was doing the best she knew how as a parent and I was doing the best I knew how when I became a parent. Sometimes the way we learn priceless lessons is quite expensive. But now that I understand just how much the things I say and do can shape a young child's life, and therefore, future, and that I have no control over how the child chooses to learn from or respond to my actions or what I say, I have become all the more careful of how I impact not only my own children but other people. Though I always knew what I did had an impact on others, I had no idea how far the ripple of my actions could travel.

# A LESSON FROM EDDIE

*"Live as if you were to die tomorrow.
Learn as if you were to live forever."*

~ Mahatma Gandhi

What if we are all really doing the best we can?

I believe most people are doing the best they can, with what they have. The effort they are putting forth is what they have the capacity to give at that moment. Their awareness of the world around them and what they know is what determines this capacity.

As for my family, I honestly believe my wife and I have done the best job we could at raising our children. Could we have done better? Maybe. But it's always after the fact that we realize the mistakes we've made; still, realizing we made a mistake gives us the opportunity to correct it and continue.

Even though I understand most people are doing the best they can, I've still spent the majority of my life judging others' abilities and capacity to perform or simply to be against how I might perform or be. Because I have often been hard on myself, it has been easy to be critical of others.

If most people are genuinely doing the best job they can at that moment given their circumstances, then shouldn't that give me permission to accept them and the contributions they are able to make?

I once was taught a similar principle by a friend who is an incredible fly fisherman. I thought I was a pretty competent fly fisherman until I became friends with Eddie, and learned there was so much more to learn—so, so much more! A whole new world of possibility opened up to me. I discovered a depth to fishing I had never known existed prior to learning from him, and my ability to appreciate fly fishing was enhanced.

Eddie taught me that as long as I have a fly that reasonably represents a food source in the water, the fish will always take it. With one condition, I must present that fly in a way that it looks real to the fish.

Before I met Eddie, I had thought that when I didn't catch fish it was mostly because of the fly I'd chosen. I would then change out one fly after another, over and over, trying to get the right fly for that fish, that time of year, that time of day, that part of the river or whatever particular area I was in—the whole time not realizing I had a big flaw in my presentation.

Eddie looked at me one day and said, "Sean, do you think a fish has a choice of what to eat and what not to eat?"

"Sure he does," I replied.

"Really? Do you really think that?"

"Sure I do. He wants the tastier looking bug." I said with a smile.

# A Lesson From Eddie

Eddie looked up at me patiently with a grin on his face. "What you're telling me is that the fish has the ability to decide when to eat this kind of bug or that kind of bug. So, you're saying the fish thinks like you and can make the decision, 'Nah, I think I'll pass on this one; there will be a better one in a few minutes,' just like you'd say, 'I don't want a bologna sandwich because I'm going to save room for a big juicy hamburger later.' No way! He doesn't know when the next bug might come floating by; it might be a while and he can't risk going hungry. Instinct kicks in so he has *no choice!*"

I started laughing, thinking about the fish deciding to get a nice juicy hamburger. The ridiculousness of that image helped me to understand instantly a simple principle that had escaped me all these years. I realized that I had essentially been projecting my thoughts onto the fish, and by extension, upon other people, which is silly.

To prove his point, Eddie took me to a small river where he had me hold a wire mesh screen in the river where a lot of rocks were upstream. He then churned up the rocks just three feet upstream from the wire mesh screen.

"Now lift it out of the water," he said, "and bring it over here to the shore."

He then showed me all the food for a fish that was in that river. Bugs I'd never seen were included among bugs with which I was quite familiar. One of them was a large Golden Stone Fly Nymph.

"Now that's funny," Eddie said with a grin. "Everybody says there's no Golden Stone Flies in this river, yet now we know differently. As a matter of fact, there are literally dozens of options here to choose from that will work great."

He then went on to teach me a great lesson to improve my presentation.

Prior to that, I'd been doing the best I knew how. Little did I know at the time that I'd been missing some wonderful information. I'd just assumed I knew what I was doing, and when it didn't work, I just tried harder and harder with the wrong information. Albert Einstein defined insanity as, "doing the same thing over and over again and expecting different results." In other words, what Eddie taught me that day was that what may fix most of the errors or wrong thinking in my life is better information.

If we're all doing our best with what we know or have been given, then what it means is I should accept everyone's offering as his or her best. The best part of this understanding is that it gives me incredible latitude to forgive what I might otherwise perceive as mistakes, poor effort, or even offenses. It helps me to accept my own past offerings rather than hate myself for "falling short" or "not measuring up." Life is full of lessons, and like everyone else, I'm still learning.

# A KEY CALLED FORGIVENESS

*"The weak can never forgive.*
*Forgiveness is the attribute of the strong."*

~ Mahatma Gandhi

How can I forgive myself? How do we forgive someone who has left us behind? How do we forgive a loved one who has wronged us? How do we forgive a friend who offends us or hurts us deeply? How do I forgive my son, who, in a moment, turned our lives upside down forever and hurt his family? Just when things started looking a little better for us as a family and we felt our burdens start to lift, just when the dawn was getting brighter, Canyon tore our lives apart by taking his own.

I've seen how pain caused by frustration and anger toward another can stop a person's progress and limit his or her happiness. It was easy to see that pain when I observed it in others. But I've also experienced it firsthand in my own life, and it was not easy to see or understand when it was me personally who was not forgiving.

What is forgiveness, and how do I apply it in my life? How do I offer forgiveness when I feel so terribly wronged? Who is there to help me through this journey? Who or what can sooth this pain?

Without forgiveness, we are stuck. We cannot move forward toward joy and happiness because the effect of not forgiving stops our progress; we are unable to see the truth in our actions. If we are devoid of forgiveness, we fail to see the damage we are doing to our own souls from things like resentment and hate or guilt and shame.

Think of it this way: If I choose to continue to drive with the front window of my car fogged up, I'm not only a danger to myself and those in my vehicle, but to others as well. I might be able to see when my window is foggy, but my vision is impaired, and I cannot trust my reactions as a result. If I defog the window, however, I will be able to see clearly and won't endanger myself or others. When I fail to forgive, my vision remains obstructed by resentment, just like that fogged-up window.

As I healed from the loss of my son, I found myself looking for answers to questions I didn't have before. After Canyon died, something inside me stopped working. My heart seemed to shut down for a while to avoid an overload of pain, fear, and conflict. Sometimes his death didn't seem real; it was difficult to feel any emotion—good or bad—at those times. At other times, the pain was so intense that I wanted to run from the engulfing flames that seemed eager to consume me in my grief.

I was hard on myself for feeling the various emotions I felt. I had a difficult time forgiving myself, even though

# A Key Called Forgiveness

I wasn't clear on what I needed to forgive myself for, if for anything. Through accepting myself, embracing who I was, and moving through the experience—even though I felt it might destroy me—I grew.

What helped me forgive was a belief in a God who loves me and is quick to forgive me. A belief in a God who laid out a just plan and provided a Savior to take on all the burdens, pains, injustices, and mistakes that I would ever experience or make. Why wouldn't a loving God be able and willing to forgive me quickly and unconditionally?

It is everyone's journey to figure out the best way to forgive and be forgiven. Personally, I find it harder to forgive myself than to forgive others. I seem to be much harder on myself than I am on others, even those who have wronged me deeply.

What would happen if we gave everyone the benefit of the doubt, including ourselves, and recognized that when someone wrongs us, it is more about that person than about us? Obviously, coming to that understanding is much easier said than done and quite contrary to human nature, but still, what if?

Maybe when we don't fully forgive, it's often because we feel as though forgiving people is "letting them off of the hook," or that we've "earned the right" to feel sorry for ourselves. But when I hold onto resentment, it punishes no one really except myself. If I'm holding on to some type of resentment, guilt, or shame toward myself and am unwilling to forgive myself, then am I not hurting myself even more?

Forgiveness gives us the ability to see the beauty that was there all along. Forgiveness allows me to love others and myself the way they and I deserve. Forgiveness open hearts and allows hope into our lives.

My son wronged my family, his friends, himself, and me. Yet, I was so quick to forgive him. I have a tremendous love for Canyon and want him to know that. The only way I can show that love and prove it is if I quickly and unconditionally forgive him.

Some people struggle with this concept of forgiveness. I understand those feelings. I've doubted these beliefs and found I had to challenge them at times. I can only say that my greatest comfort has come from a belief in God and the feelings of peace I have received as a result, so I suggest them to you as a way to heal from any pain.

I know a woman who is incredibly blessed, but never happy. Like many we all know, she is surrounded by blessings, but she doesn't see them because she is so focused on injustices. She blames. She is a perpetual victim. The root of her pain is that she can't seem to forgive the wrongs that have been committed against her. She refuses to acknowledge that she plays a part in her own misery. If she could truly forgive, she could enjoy the bright dawn of a brilliant new day.

By forgiving those she blames, she might realize that nothing from her past has the power to write her future, unless she gives it the power. Through forgiveness, her life could be joyful and full of blessings. Her capacity to love would multiply. She could immediately see more of life's rewards rather than only what she doesn't want in her life.

I must forgive those who have wronged me in any way. I must forgive them for what they did and any pain they might

# A Key Called Forgiveness

have caused the ones I love or me. This forgiveness includes those who left me or abandoned me in any way. I must forgive myself for anything I should have done or said, but didn't. I must forgive myself for the anger and resentment I have felt at times. I must acknowledge that all these feelings are normal, and I'm not a bad person for having had them. None of this pain is worth holding onto. To do so is like trying to walk through mud with a ball and chain around my ankle. Get rid of the pain of hate, resentment, guilt, or shame. They are corrosive emotions, eating away at our lives and stopping us from becoming whom we are meant to be.

Sometimes we don't even know what or who we are not forgiving or even why we have the resentment we do; we are just stuck. I could give a lot of advice on the technique of how to forgive, but it's so much easier said than done. There are emotional clearing techniques, counseling experts, and endless books and resources. It seems more and more that this space is being filled with what I call noise. Noise, because it's so difficult to get through; it's difficult to hear through all the noise, especially for someone who really needs to heal. The reason for this noise is because there is so much pain in the world. So many people want to heal, need to heal, and deserve to heal.

Forgiveness is at the root of all healing. The single greatest way to forgive is to let go. Make a conscious decision that it's not doing you any good to hold onto the pain and resentment, and let go. Trust that a loving God has provided a way for all things to be made right, and although we may not understand it, we must let go, or we are stopping our own eternal progress and happiness.

# LOVE LEAVENS

*"I honestly do not know if love vanquishes death
as our traditional faiths teach,
but I do know that our vulnerabilities
trump our ideologies
and that love leavens
the purity and logic of our beliefs,
propelling us to connect
as the fiercely gracious human beings we are."*

~ Rabbi Irwin Kula

AFTER CANYON DIED, SOME PEOPLE AVOIDED the situation all together. I don't blame or judge them. I wonder how many times I've been in a similar situation when I could have helped someone gather courage in his or her loss, but I chose instead to stay away from the burning fires of sorrow. Some of my best friends and family are among those who never reached out. I cannot judge them, but I wonder whether their inability to step into the fire of our sorrow with us was because of my personality and their belief that I'd rather be left alone. Had my message become "I can handle all of my own stuff" over the years?

It was another tragedy that I didn't easily accept help. I was reluctant to risk being seen as needing help. I now realize that was a weakness in me. Shame on me for setting up that scenario, if that's the case. If someone feels guilty for not being there, I hope this shows my insight into my failings. I thought I had to be strong and keep myself together. Society teaches men that they shouldn't ask for, or accept, help from others, and anyone who does so isn't a "real" man.

Letting go of the need to be something I'm not has made my load lighter. The truly heavy burdens in life, the ones that aren't easily set down, aren't easier to bear if you're strong physically or emotionally. They're easier to bear if you're humble and acknowledge that you are (like everyone else) weak in many ways. The load becomes lighter when you realize and accept that you won't always be strong enough to keep it together, and that's okay.

It takes a lot of strength to seem invincible, but it takes even more strength to be vulnerable. As a matter of fact, you may be your strongest and most invincible when you are most vulnerable because that's when you tend to recognize your weaknesses, thereby, allowing you to accept help. These times of truth are when others get the opportunity to reach out and help.

After Canyon's death, not only did I have to face the loss of my son, but I also faced a new way of interacting with others. I feared others would judge me or think less of me. I worried people would think I was a terrible, defective father because I had a son who shot himself. Over time, I realized it didn't really matter what people might assume about me.

Fortunately, the reality is that most people we knew were (and are) kind and gracious. They don't seem quick to jump to negative conclusions, but rather, they have empathy for what a difficult situation it was (and is) for my family.

In retrospect, if I could give a younger version of me some advice, I would tell him to love himself and worry less about what others think. I would tell him to worry less about having to be the guy in charge, the guy who's in control, the guy who has it all together. There are more important things in life than being tough and strong. Let others love and help you.

The evening Canyon died, I was weak and helpless. All my defenses were down. A bomb had gone off in the center of my universe, taking any pride or ego I'd had with it. It was purely survival for my family and me. I was naked to the world, totally exposed and feeling unsafe. I would have taken a long hug from anyone who offered it, and I did. I would have let anyone hold me, because I needed it so badly. I needed to hear it would be okay—and that I was okay. I needed to hear that someone believed in me and had my back. Days later, as I was regaining my strength, my defenses started to come up again, and it became more difficult for me to show my vulnerability.

The evening of Canyon's death, I let a neighbor hold me as we sat together on the floor. I sat there hugging my knees to my chest as tears flowed at an uncontrollable rate. My chest ached and I could hardly breathe. My neighbor put his arms around me and held me tight. He cried as he told me he didn't know what to do for me, but he was there for me. He truly didn't know what to do, no one did, but he had no fear, or he had made the decision that helping me was more important than his fear. He was clearly more concerned about helping me than he was about any awkwardness he might have had about not knowing me enough to be the one to console me the way he was. I admire Dave for his courage and heart, for his ability to be such a huge man and put himself out there for me that night. We didn't know each other particularly well, but it didn't matter.

The sad thing was that my pride wouldn't allow me to continue to let him be there for me as I tried to settle into my comfort zone over the next few weeks. Dave was still there, but when the shock and gut-wrenching pain of the tragedy was over, it wasn't as easy for either of us to extend ourselves. We still admire each other dearly, he for my courage and me for his. Dave is just one example. Many others put their arms around me and pulled me into their hearts. Some said profound things that I marveled at and found truly comforting. Others said precious little or just told me they loved and cared for me. Even those simple words brought healing and reassurance.

Cards trickled in from people telling us how important we were in their lives and how sorry they were for our loss. Some wrote at length, others just wrote three simple words, "We love you." All had a profound way of making us feel loved and encouraged.

The women of our neighborhood got together and put a cooler on our front porch. Each evening for almost three weeks, dinner was in that cooler every night. We never had to think about what to cook. This gesture was a tremendous help to Cologne and I, who didn't have to worry about what to fix for dinner, so instead, we could focus on other needs, and as a result, the entire family felt better.

Sometimes, these tender mercies came in the form of a random phone call. "Just checking on you. We want you to know we care. How are you doing? How can I help?"

Some of the most meaningful acts of love and kindness came when friends, family, or neighbors didn't ask what they could do or what we needed. Instead, they recognized a need, stepped in, and gracefully helped meet that need. They showed no fear and helped lighten our sorrow with their love.

Marianne Williamson, in her book *A Return to Love*, said:

> Our deepest fear is not that we are inadequate. Our deepest fear is that we are powerful beyond measure. It is our light, not our darkness that most frightens us. We ask ourselves, Who am I to be brilliant, gorgeous, talented, and fabulous? Actually, who are you not to be? You are a child of God. Your playing small does not serve the world. There is nothing enlightened about shrinking so that other people won't feel insecure around you. We are all meant to shine, as children do. We were born to make manifest the glory of God that is within us. It's not just in some of us; it's in everyone. And, as we let our own light shine, we unconsciously give other people permission to do the same. As we are liberated from our own fear, our presence automatically liberates others.

What incredible examples our friends and family were to us at that time of the lesson described in this quote. I will be forever impressed with the love, care, compassion, and acts of goodwill showered upon us in our time of need. I know many people didn't receive an adequate "Thank you," but I hope they know how much we appreciate them to this day. Thank you for being so courageous, so vulnerable, and for giving so much of yourselves. Thank you for letting your light shine in our darkest hour and helping to light our way.

# FORT BUILDING
# & COURAGE

*"Anything worth doing is worth doing poorly . . . at first."*

~ Keith Cunningham

"Anything worth doing is worth doing well." Most of us have heard this over and over and taken this adage as a lesson when we were children. Today we try to follow it as we go about life's tasks. I took this lesson seriously, too seriously, actually. It's always been important for me to do my best at any task I set out to accomplish, from building a tree fort when I was a kid to building a home when I was older. Since our skills change vastly over the years, I know I could build one heck of a tree fort now!

Because I've taken this "Do It Well" lesson to heart over the years, sometimes to my detriment, I've avoided things I don't know how to do. In other words, I don't start because I'm afraid I won't know how to do that particular task. If I don't know how to do it, then there's a good chance I won't do it well. And with what I learned all those years ago, there's now a little pesky voice inside my head that constantly reminds me: Anything worth doing is worth doing well.

Grief has been the same type of process. I didn't know what I was doing, or how to do it "right." No one had ever shown me how to grieve the "right way" (as if there is such a thing). My grief process was raw and disrupting, but I had no choice—I was thrown into it. Not knowing what to do with my feelings, I held them back and didn't let anyone see them. I told myself there would be a time when I would be better at grieving, and then I would share my emotions.

Whether this decision was conscious or not, it was the result of my conditioning and life experience. I just didn't have the faith required to lean forward and be vulnerable when I was in such deep pain. Not only that, but I'd learned early on (as most men do) to keep my feelings to myself because sharing them caused me more pain and made me look weak.

When I was a kid, I wasn't afraid to build a tree fort. I didn't know how to do it, but that didn't stop me. The fort looked horrible, but that had nothing to do with anything I was concerned with at the time. I was concerned with one thing: The process of having fun, of enjoying life. And although I didn't know it at the time, I was learning. It wasn't until someone told me, "Your tree fort is stupid" that I got uneasy about it. If I'd only known that a tree fort doesn't have a brain, and therefore can't be "stupid," I would have had a great comeback, but I didn't make the connection. The barb just sat inside me, and as it sat, it festered. What I heard was, "You are stupid."

The criticism hurt me, but all of a sudden, I cared a

little more about what my tree fort looked like. Some of the fun was now gone from the process, and I was a little more concerned how I did it the next time. I lost some more of my childlike innocence and play was not as easy.

I suppose life's harshest critics can ultimately help us learn, and many mean well, but it's curious to me how children are willing to be totally authentic and vulnerable before they start to lose that innocence of not knowing any better. If we could all be a little more childlike at times, we might find we have less fear. If we could have that innocence and willingness to be authentic and vulnerable, our newfound abilities would create a powerful combination for success.

Canyon had a childlike quality, even as he got older, and I aspire to his ability to be so authentic and vulnerable. This quality and ability taught me many lessons. One such time was when he decided to play hockey.

# COURAGE SCORES BIG

I walk through the front door of my home and into the family room after a long day at work. Cologne and Canyon are leaning over a very large duffle bag on the floor in the middle of the room. Shoulder pads and gear are inside the bag and spread out on the floor. By the corner of the couch are hockey skates and a hockey stick.

"Hello," I say as I walk into the room. "This looks fun; what's up?"

They both look at me with big smiles, and Cologne proudly announces, "Canyon decided to play hockey and is signed up to play for the high school hockey team. His first practice is tonight. Isn't that great?"

I feel my face tighten. My heart sinks and I'm confused. 'Are you crazy?' goes through my head. I try to show excitement because if he's really decided to play hockey, I want to be his biggest fan and support him with everything I've got; I don't want him to think otherwise.

"Really? That's cool, Canyon! I didn't know you liked hockey. How'd you decide to play hockey?"

"Mom told me that Julia, your assistant, wanted me to be on the team and it sounded like fun."

"I didn't know the high school had a hockey team."

"It's not an official sponsored team; it's more like a club, but they play other high schools," Canyon answers.

"Cool," I say, and try to sound confident.

My brain is conflicted and I'm wondering who to pin to the wall, Julia or Cologne. Who talked my son who hasn't played team sports since T-ball and a bout of soccer when he was eight, into playing one of the toughest sports there is? 'Why don't we just rub lamb's blood all over him and throw him to the wolves?' is the question that pounds in my head, but I can't ask it.

I spend a few minutes looking over the expensive gear. It's really cool, and if I had been in his shoes, I'd be really excited.

"I always wanted to play hockey, Canyon, but they didn't have high school hockey when I was in school, and we didn't have enough money for me to play on the city league team.

## Fort Building & Courage

This is really cool! Are you sure you want to play hockey, though? It's a pretty rough sport."

"Yeah, it sounds like fun," he says with a big grin on his face.

"How much did all this gear cost?" I ask, then gaze at Cologne and wait for an answer.

"A little more than seven-hundred dollars," she replies.

My stomach goes weak and a little green, but I try hard to act as though it's no big deal. A thought has been playing ping-pong inside my head. This could go wrong in so many ways. Bouncing back and forth, the thought won't quit, so I have to get it out.

"Cologne, can I talk to you for a minute?"

We walk into the bedroom and leave Canyon playing with his cool new gear.

"WHAT ARE YOU THINKING?" are the first words that fly out of my mouth in a loud whisper as soon as the bedroom door closes. "DO YOU KNOW ANYTHING ABOUT HOCKEY? Have you ever seen a hockey game?"

"Well, no .... Why are you so upset?" she asks, sounding disappointed.

"Because you just threw our son to the wolves."

"What are you talking about? Julia said he'd love it, and they need players," she proclaims.

"Cologne, I'll bet if you can lace your skates, you can play hockey for the club team. Canyon has been ice skating one time. He spent most of his time on his butt, and he's not even good at roller blading. You know he's not athletic. Hockey is an extremely rough sport. It's the only sport where the referees don't stop the fights. Hockey is the sport tough kids who want to beat on people play. What makes you think I want my son getting the crap knocked out of him?"

"Oh my gosh, I didn't know! Julia said he'd . . . ."

The look on Cologne's face is one of deep concern.

"What did Julia say? How did she talk you two into this?" I ask, frustrated with both my office assistant and my wife.

"She asked me what he liked to do. I told her he likes video games and chess. She told me hockey is fast-paced like video games, and that it involves a lot of strategy, sort of like chess."

I sit down on the bed with my head in my hands. I'm frustrated with my assistant, Julia, who never talked with me about this, so I feel like she betrayed me. I don't know whether I should put a stop to the whole thing or let it play out.

"You know we are not going to be able to return that gear after he quits next week," I say.

"Oh my gosh, what are we going to do? What did I do? He's so excited," she says.

"I'm going to fire Julia, to start with." The words spit out of my mouth.

"No, Sean. She meant well. Let him try it. I really think Canyon will like it."

That evening, Kevin and I are sitting in the bleachers at a city ice rink. Players from the hockey team start shooting out onto the ice, one after another. As they charge onto the ice from the tunnel below the bleachers, there is energy and a power that smells tough (well, it stinks like a locker room).

It's raw and exciting, though—a thick, mesmerizing energy. Kevin is filled with awe; so am I. The players skate around the ice with a combination of power and grace.

My trance ends when I realize I don't see my son. I wonder where he is. Then Kevin says, "There's Canyon." I look down at the tunnel where Kevin is pointing. The rest of the boys had just shot out like darts onto the ice from the same place. Canyon stands there on the edge of the ice, looking wobbly and talking to one of the assistant coaches I'd just met.

The two of them edge slowly out onto the ice. Canyon, wobbly and timid on blades, and the coach in his street shoes. They cross the rink to the other side. Canyon is all padded up in his new gear and looks a hundred pounds heavier than normal. He only weighs about 130 pounds as it is, and some guys on the team have to be 200 pounds or more. I swallow a big gulp in my chest and hate myself for letting this moment happen. I see that Kevin has fixed his gaze on his older brother, wondering what's going to happen next. Kevin's mouth is wide open as he leans forward on the edge of his seat.

I have a lump stuck in my throat, and not the good kind. I hurt for my son and the lesson he is going to get. I've always tried to set up wins for my children. It's my opinion that all kids need more successes in life. I don't see this turning out well.

The coach is standing in front of Canyon, just inches from his face; he's talking to Canyon through his face mask; Canyon is nodding, and it looks as if each nod of his head might knock him off balance.

Kevin looks up at me to see whether I'm watching this too; then he quickly turns back to watch Canyon.

When the coach walks to the side wall, Canyon turns around to face the other direction. His feet shoot out from under him, and he falls flat on his back. Kevin bursts out laughing. Canyon quickly gets up and starts to skate forward toward the opposite wall.

The whole team is on the other end of the ice and working hard with the coaches. A lot of noise and energy pulsates from that end of the ice. They are doing drills. Stopping and starting quickly. Steel and ice are scraping and clashing together. The sound is intense and intimidating. These boys look like they must have been born on the ice.

Back on this end of the ice, Canyon has fallen a few more times trying to do what the coach is asking him to do. Kevin is laughing at this tragedy as only a young boy can. He's fallen off the seat and is holding his gut like it hurts, but he can't stop laughing. He's under my feet. I push my heel against him, push him further under my seat, and say, "Quiet. Quiet!" He belly laughs some more, and then I lose it and snort out a short burst of laughter.

Canyon can't hear us. I don't want him to. He is very intent on what he is doing. Now two coaches are working with him and they have put some orange cones out. Canyon is getting a crash course in skating. It's beyond funny. It's hilarious. Kevin won't stop laughing; he gets louder every time Canyon falls. I'm trying desperately not to let Kevin make a scene, and I laugh myself at times, but inside I'm really crying.

# Fort Building & Courage

How can Canyon be so brave to try something so new, so out of his element, not to mention face the potential ridicule? Isn't he concerned about how he looks? Isn't he afraid of being embarrassed in front of so many people?

The coaches are working him hard. He's doing better, but he's far from being either graceful or powerful. At the opposite end of the ice, one of the boys just stops every once in awhile and watches Canyon. I notice some boys laugh from time to time, but the coaches keep them engaged and working hard.

Practice continues. Canyon never puts a stick in his hands the entire practice. They just work on skating skills. I don't remember Kevin ever having laughed so hard. It's innocent, and it stops about halfway through after I remind him he wouldn't like it if that were him out there, and we were laughing at him. As for me, I have a full range of emotions I can hardly describe. I feel so bad for Canyon. The coaches have worked him hard. He's fallen on his back, on his face, and on his side. He's hit the ice repeatedly. He has to be exhausted, bruised, and beaten up. It's been difficult to watch. I know his hockey playing days will be over the moment he gets in the car. He is going to quit. I start to imagine advertising his hockey gear in the newspaper at half price because he has used it and we can no longer return it.

After practice, Kevin and I are sitting in the car when Canyon walks up. I've asked Kevin to say only good things. Canyon throws his gear in the back and gets in the front seat, exhausted.

"Wow," he says. "That was hard! I can't wait until next week."

"Really? Well, okay then—I'm glad you liked it." I am still concerned, but with that type of response, what else can I do other than support him with everything I have?

"Man, you sure were good at falling," Kevin says with a big grin on his face as he leans over the front seat.

"I know, huh, but it was fun," Canyon says with a smile.

A different type of respect and bond seems to go through Kevin as he looks at the older brother he laughed at earlier.

Playing on the hockey team was good for Canyon. I figured it would be a difficult experience for him, but he stuck with it. He wasn't good, but he loved it. He kept showing up, and he kept getting a little better. He wasn't powerful and he wasn't graceful, but he never quit.

Scoring a goal in hockey is not an easy task. That's why there isn't a lot of scoring during a game. Kids go years without scoring a goal. So when Canyon scored a goal several weeks after that first practice, the whole world seemed to pause for a brief moment. He was so excited! The whole team was excited! The opposing team couldn't figure out what all the fuss was about. It was just a goal, after all, and a lucky one at that. But the luck of it wasn't what made it special. It was that the kid who didn't play sports, didn't know how to skate just weeks ago, and barely knew how to lace his skates would not be denied. He had made a decision and didn't quit. Because Canyon scored a goal, the world stood still for an instant to celebrate the sheer joy of what had just happened.

After scoring the goal, Canyon was so excited that he skated up to the glass where we were sitting, and in his state of pure happiness, he didn't even pay attention to what was going on around him. The referee didn't want him or the team to celebrate so enthusiastically, but Canyon's entire team was going nuts.

I'll never forget seeing Canyon, his face right up at the glass, yelling through the glass with his mouth guard still in his mouth, preventing him from being understood. "I scored a goal! I scored a goal! Did you see that? I scored a goal!"

No one could understand him because he was mumbling behind his mouth guard and the glass, but everyone knew what he was saying.

He was just being Canyon. We loved it and were very proud of him.

The team gave him the puck from his goal. They made him feel like he had just scored the winning goal of a championship game. He treasured it. He was hooked. It was official; he loved hockey.

---

Canyon played one full season before he died. He was never great, but he loved it. Even more important, he never quit. I learned some valuable lessons from my son the day he scored that goal. I still have the puck, and I'll always have the feeling.

# FAITH AND COURAGE

Do little children already have faith, or is there something especially innocent about them where faith is not required so that they are able to do courageous things? I don't know the answer, but I do know that most of us don't get to continue to operate in innocence much after our youngest years. When innocence leaves, it means I need a new tool to help me make decisions that something else is greater than what I fear.

For some reason, Canyon was able to continue to operate in a childlike innocence for a long time into his teenage years. I was not so fortunate, so for me, at least, the tool to help me have greater courage is faith.

Faith is required for courage to exist; the two work in tandem. My level of courage expands as my faith causes me to act. As my level of faith expands, I get to exercise a new level of faith and the cycle continues.

We all have a need to learn and grow. It's a bit of a mess for me to comprehend, sometimes, but it's a powerful principle. Anytime I take action in an unknown area, I act because of faith. This action moves into (and sometimes beyond) the barrier of my known experience into the unknown experience, and again, it requires faith and courage to expand further. All mastery, sacrifice, abundance, discovery, risk, growth, and new possibilities lie beyond the barrier of my known experiences. Because I have experienced loss, I now have a new level of knowledge and awareness. Just as faith and courage were required for Canyon to score a goal in hockey and have the wonderful experience he had, so faith and courage are required to survive the lessons learned in any kind of loss.

# GRATITUDE - A MASTER KEY

*"Gratitude is not only the greatest of virtues,*

*but the parent of all others."*

~ Cicero

A COACH ONCE CHALLENGED ME TO GO A WEEK without complaining. Just one short week. How hard could it be? All I had to do was last seven days. I couldn't get upset with myself if I messed up because that would void the challenge too. If I did, he said, no big deal. I could just start over again. I thought to myself, "No problem! I can do this."

Well, the truth is it took me about seven weeks to go one week. Then I asked myself, "Could I go another week?" Eventually, I went thirty days without complaining, although it was difficult.

Something magical happened to me during that time. I started to realize all the things I had complained about before were likely there to provide me a lesson, something that could make me a better person. I became more aware of the little things that had bothered me before and were no longer important. What was the lesson in each?

I also became cognizant of how much everyone criticizes and finds fault with others and themselves. Yet, I became more patient with the people I encountered, and as a result, I was treated better for the way I communicated with them.

I often found myself lifting the spirits of someone who was experiencing a bad day, and through the process, even I felt better! As a society, we've grown accustomed to everyone's complaints, and many of us are on the defensive as a result. We're afraid of criticism, so we don't do or say as much as we could because our subconscious defense system is protecting us from others' complaints. By not allowing myself to complain, I transformed my way of thinking, and those around me are better off for it.

Although I didn't speak to others about my little challenge, interestingly enough, people around me started to take on the same trait and not complain as much, either. People tend not to complain as much when the people around them don't whine or commiserate with them. I'm not suggesting you shouldn't grieve with those who are genuinely grieving or help those who are in trouble. I'm talking about whining and pointless complaining, like the woman who says, every day, "This coffee is never hot enough," or the friend who constantly tells you his boss is a jerk. And there's the person in your carpool who says, "Will you look at that idiot? No one knows how to drive these days." Watch what happens when you don't play into that critical attitude. It's just not as much fun to complain when nobody complains with you. You feel out of place whining about something trivial when others don't participate. My family benefited the most from this exercise, and I have noticed that they complain much less now too.

Of course, this challenge needs to come with a disclaimer that none of us are perfect. We are still learning and exercising the muscles needed to change our patterns. The longer I practice this exercise, the more I am aware of the difference it makes and the more enjoyable and rewarding my life becomes. I also believe its purpose is something I can quickly lose sight of; it's easy to fall back into my old pattern of viewing the world with an eye toward finding something wrong.

For example, I slacked off for a while and was right back to complaining at different times. I heard myself saying things I couldn't believe I'd said. I literally said, "I can't believe I just said that . . . ." after making a negative statement about someone or something.

Staying in an attitude of gratitude and giving up whining and complaining is not a natural process. It goes directly against human nature because it is so much easier to complain. It requires us to be consciously aware of what we feel, do, and say. It's a choice. I hope there will come a time in my life when being grateful and complaint-free is an unconscious act. I look forward to when that happens; I strive toward it, but my guess is I will always have to make an effort to maintain and improve my ability to remain grateful. Still, it's a fun challenge, and it's worth the effort.

I also believe that if I'm a chronic complainer, I may be addicted to my problems. I know this sounds horrible and somewhat crazy, but we actually like our problems. Even worse, we love our problems. We need our problems at times as a child needs a comfort blanket or special stuffed animal. We get something out of our problems, just like an alcoholic gets something from a drink. Our problems can give us a physiological rush just as drugs or alcohol do with an addict.

Since we need to have our "fix" of problems, something to make us unhappy so we can complain, we unconsciously go around creating more problems. That way, we'll have something to slow us down and feed our "problem-dependent" personalities. If we always have problems, we never have to accept full responsibility for what happens in our lives. We become victims, held back by the very problems we subconsciously seek. The victim mentality, in which everything that happens to us is bad, caused by outside forces, or beyond our control, is prevalent in our society today. Those who have this mind-set never lack someone or something to blame for their problems. They never have to take responsibility for their actions, because—as they see it—they're not the ones who control their lives; the weather, another person, a job, or money puts them where they are, and they're not responsible for it. "Victims" fear responsibility because taking responsibility forces them to go "cold turkey," leaving them unable to blame others or the environment for what's wrong in their lives.

Through the loss of my son, I learned about the "blame game" victims play. Of course, I wish Canyon were still here and that the tragedy of his loss had never occurred. But I didn't have a choice. It happened and Canyon is gone. However, I do have a choice in the aftermath. I can take on the victim mentality or I can look for what possible good could come out of this horrific experience. As someone who has been there, I choose to focus on how I might possibly help others who are grieving.

I cannot change the fact that my son is gone, and I cannot change the way it happened. It is a part of my life, so at times I will need to talk about it or share my feelings with others. I cannot change that such sharing makes me feel vulnerable. I cannot change that two of my children were the ones who found him. I cannot change that Canyon's friends continue to grow, have lives, and even start families of their own, while my son isn't here to share their experiences, and his own, with them. I won't get to watch and enjoy Canyon grow into a man. I cannot change that when he was alive, I did and said things I regret. I cannot change the horror of that evening. I cannot change the unspeakable tragedy of losing a beloved child. I cannot change that I don't have all the answers.

If those factors are out of my control, what can I change? What can I choose? What is within my ability to control? I can change the way I view his death. I can choose the way I remember him. I can recognize the value of the time I had with him. I can change the way I treat those I love. I can change the way I communicate with those I love. I can change the things I didn't like about myself before he died, prideful things about me that didn't serve anyone. I can choose to focus on my happy memories of time spent with Canyon. These memories are just as valid as the memories that hurt, and a lot healthier to dwell on.

I can choose to recognize the blessings in my life. I can choose to realize that my life doesn't revolve around me and my needs, and I can recognize the collective experience that transcends my own. I can choose what I focus on. I can choose to value the gifts that have come about because of my increased awareness. I can choose to honor Canyon's legacy. I can choose to remember everything I did right during the time he graced this world with his presence. I can choose to see his face and contagious smile in my mind's eye. I can choose to help others who have gone through loss and can't see their way out. I can recognize everything for which I am grateful. I can change the way I live.

I had an incredible experience one evening after I had gone through the exercise of being grateful. I retired to bed for the evening at about eleven o'clock. I was in a grateful state and quite relaxed—but unable to sleep. I remember thinking I would just lay there, relaxed, and instead of being frustrated and upset because I couldn't sleep, I'd be grateful for the warm bed and the opportunity to rest my body. As I pondered these things, I thought of my son and how grateful I was for the time I had with him. I don't know how long I lay there, but I was about to fall asleep when his entire life started to play in my mind, as if it were a movie. It started as just a flash of pictures and memories of experiences we had while he was alive. Then I recognized that I had received a gift of memory outside of my normal capacity. It was one of the most beautiful and spiritual experiences that has ever happened to me. I wept a constant flow of tears as these amazing tender memories continued to flow, a steady, unbroken stream from Heaven.

I lay on my back with my eyes closed and tried to be silent so I wouldn't wake my wife. I didn't want this cascade of memories to stop, and if Cologne woke and asked why I was crying, it might end. Tears ran down my face and into my ears. Those tears pooled behind my ears, then broke through my hairline and ran down my scalp and onto the pillow, this didn't matter. I was engaged in the most intense visual dream I'd ever experienced. It filled my whole soul with a joy, a feeling of inexpressible gratitude. As it concluded, I felt I knew my son better than I did when he was alive. I cherished my experiences with him even more. I sat up in bed and realized that my pillow was soaked in tears like someone had poured a glass of water on it. I looked at the clock on my dresser; it read 4:00 a.m. This experience had gone on for over four hours and was all about my memories of my son, who was so grateful himself, and our life together. I got a new pillow and fell sound asleep because I was exhausted from the experience.

I believe this gift I had been given came from my ability to be grateful. Although I believe the memories were divinely retrieved and given as a gift I needed at that time, those memories were stored in my own mind.

I may not have had the capacity to retrieve those memories on my own, but they were there the whole time. Had I been in any other state than that of complete gratitude, I don't believe I would have had this same experience. I recognize this gift may have been unique to my situation, a gift not many have or will ever experience. For this reason, it was not something I felt comfortable sharing with anyone at the time. I am sharing it now because I want you to know what incredible value and magnificent beauty is possible when we are truly grateful for life, when we can transcend the inconveniences, trials, adversity, and even loss, and recognize the true value of our experiences.

I heard someone once say that if life is not working for you and you're unhappy, sit down and make a list of two hundred things that make you grateful. Take twenty index cards and write down ten items you are grateful for per card. Don't stop until you have finished the list. This list will help you get clear on what makes you truly grateful. It may be hard to come up with this many. In fact, you may find it impossible at first, but keep going. You may get to a level that is beyond what you thought possible in the past. You may get to a level where you start crying. When you have completed the task, take these cards and keep them with you. Whenever you are unhappy, upset, or disappointed, take them out and start reading through your list. I share this process because it is how I finally got through the first thirty days without complaining. I've also benefited from a gratitude journal. Every evening for ninety days, before I fell asleep, I forced myself to write down five successes that I'd had during the day or five things I'd experienced during the day for which I was grateful. This daily assessment created a conditioning for success and gratitude and taught me to see my life differently.

In addition, I had a little exercise I enjoyed when I would run in the mornings. In the first several minutes of running, I'd think through in my mind as many things as I could for which I felt thankful. I remember having a smile on my face as I ran down the street one dark cold rainy morning, a time when I wouldn't normally be smiling. However, I was thinking of how grateful I was for paved roads and storm drainage, so all the water on the roads ran off, so the cars didn't splash as much cold water on me as they drove past. I started thinking of curbs and gutters and sewer systems, and how I get to benefit from all this great technology. That led to thoughts of concrete and asphalt and how they are made and all the reasons and details, and how what I was grateful for went down a "rabbit hole." It may be funny, but it was sincere. True, I was smiling because I was grateful, but I was also smiling because I'd reached a new level of appreciation, and because if anyone could have heard my thoughts, they might have thought I was crazy.

Though I've had some very difficult trials in my life, I don't have to look very far to find examples of people who have had trials I might perceive as impossible. Numerous incredible examples exist throughout history of men and women who have overcome incredible odds and terrible adversity. Those who end up being an inspiration to all of us are those who appreciate what they have and what they gained from their experiences.

I could create a long list of names, including Viktor Frankl, Anne Frank, and Nelson Mandela. We don't have to look very far in order to find people who have overcome what we might view as impossible hardships. Yet, they triumphed and became inspirations. Sometimes they are right beside us, people we know and care about.

Happiness in life is a function of how grateful we are and what we choose to focus on. Things don't create this happiness. Wealth doesn't do it. Friends or social status don't do it. Looks don't do it. Talk to anyone who has any or all of these in great abundance and that person will tell you their happiness is not found in these things. Sure, we can enjoy such things, as we should. But the difficulty of this illusion lies in the fact that they can go away at any moment—any of them could be gone tomorrow. If our self-worth or happiness is intertwined in any way with *things*, we will suffer greatly upon their loss.

Gratitude is a better gauge of true happiness. Gratitude transforms our lives and makes us better beings.

# MY RED-SHELL TREASURES

*"It's not what you look at that matters, it's what you see."*

~ Henry David Thoreau

I CONSIDER MYSELF A BLESSED MAN. Yet as you now know, I have not always been good at recognizing my blessings. Sometimes the treasures were right in front of me, but I was too busy or distracted to see them. Sometimes I even trampled them under my feet, unaware of what was there. I can say that my family is one of those treasures—especially my dear wife, Cologne. She is the hero of my story. She is the one who deserves center stage. Some of the scenes in our life have been dark and terrible, but most have been stunning and bright. When the final curtain falls, and the cast is announced, I want to make sure she is the lead, that she gets the credit. Her capacity to love and stick by her family has breathed life into our children and me. Yes, she suffered tremendously and yes, some of the suffering caused regretful decisions. If we could go back and do it all over again with the knowledge we have now, I'm sure there are some things we would all do differently, even her. But she has helped to teach me through example what is the greatest treasure of all, the greatest skill I could have learned. She might even deny that she was the one who taught me this skill and instead argue that I taught her. This skill is one that everything in need of refinement must go through. It is a skill spoken of in ancient texts and yet misunderstood by many in its application to mortality. It is the skill of sitting in the refiner's fire.

No skill is more important than endurance, of being able to endure the fire, even when it becomes dangerously hot and all you want to do is run away. Peace comes in knowing that nothing in this mortal life can destroy my spirit, and that the only way I can grow and expand into a better being is through the fire of adversity and trial. All base elements can withstand the furnace's fire. Heat doesn't destroy them; it refines them and makes them better, stronger, even purer. According to a Chinese proverb, "Pure gold fears no fire." Each of us will have the opportunity to go through a refiner's fire of some kind at some time. My wife has shown me that she is able to endure a refiner's fire. She is "pure gold." That doesn't mean our journeys were necessarily graceful. It doesn't mean either of us did anything special or endured the pain, right or wrong. What it does mean is she didn't turn and run, even in her fear. She didn't quit!

She just loved, and the hotter it got, the more love she poured on the fire and on all of us. Love vanquishes all kinds of pain, including the heat of adversity. Her love was a soothing balm in the heat of our furnace, even as she was

## My Red-Shell Treasures

being transformed before our eyes, in that same heat. I often took her love for granted. I often only saw what was bothering me. Because I was distracted with the heat, at times, like the red shells in the sand, I trampled these treasures underfoot, unaware.

Just like the first night I met her, she has always inspired me. Even when I think she is not inspiring me. Even when I believe she is pushing all the wrong buttons, she is giving me an opportunity to be a better man. She may not always know it herself. She may seldom be consciously aware of it, but everything I need to be a better man I have somehow attracted in this enduring and graceful woman.

Life dealt us some difficult trials, and we lost track of each other for a while. We went through the terrible ordeal of losing our precious son. The way became cloudy and I lost track at times of who she was (and is). Then one day I turned around, and standing in front of me was the woman of my dreams, with long, dark, wavy hair and tan skin. Her dark eyes drew me in like a gravity vortex in a science fiction movie. They were deep and seemingly endless. Her smile made my knees weak and my tongue froze in my throat. I barely got out the words, "Have you been here the whole time?"

"Yes," she said with a smile, her eyes drilling into mine as all time stood still. I felt like an idiot for not recognizing her at times, and I realized I didn't care whether anyone knew I was. What mattered was that she know what a treasure she has been to me and our family.

My children have also been an incredible example to me as they have forgiven me over and over for my inability to be as aware of their needs as I might have been. They have shown me an incredible capacity to be flexible and adapt to the fire of adversity. They have grown, and they have also been transformed in the heat of this furnace. We may never fully understand or have all the answers to the questions we ask in life. Here's one I ask often: "How could I be so lucky?" And although I may never fully have an answer to this question, there is always one more thing I must say to my creator: "Thank you!"

# RETURN TO LOST CANYON

*"We find in life exactly what we put into it."*

~Ralph Waldo Emerson

---

As I walk off of the boarding ramp into the Boise Airport, I wonder what I will do for half a day while I wait for the meetings I've scheduled in the afternoon. I'll be meeting with a landowner about his property. As a commercial real estate agent, I am representing an apartment builder who is flying in later. It is Friday and I had to catch the earlier flight because it was the only one available at the last minute, but it leaves me now with several hours to fill.

I decide I will drive out to Eagle and see the old home I grew up in. It will only take me about thirty minutes to drive out there. The thought excites me as I decide to go. As I turn onto Floating Feather Road, the entire area is different from what I remember as a child.

The open farm fields of grains and alfalfa I remember are now subdivisions of very nice homes—not like the little home where I grew up. Beautiful artistic landscaping lines the border streets of these new subdivisions with rolling berms of green grass, nice trees, and manicured bushes. As I drive up to the place that used to be the long quarter mile dirt road that went to our little farmhouse, I find it is no longer accessible because of new construction. About a hundred yards from the road, the dirt driveway begins again, and from there, it still cuts through the fields back to where the big trees marked the location of the old farmhouse. I can see from that distance, however, that the three large old barns next to my home are now gone.

I drive around through the subdivisions, trying to find a new access point to my old home, but it is an unfamiliar maze. After several attempts that don't work, I have to come in from the back side, through a subdivision that was built on the property below my old home. Our little old farmhouse and barns sat on the edge of a hill that overlooked Dry Creek below. Fortunately, I am in a four-wheel drive since as I come to the hill below the old farmhouse, there is an excavation where a developer is cutting a new subdivision road up the hill to my old home.

I drive up the dirt road to the top of the hill. When I arrive at the top, I see that the two homes that used to be there are gone and so are the barns. No structures remain. What is left instead is an isolated grove of trees. They are the same trees that once surrounded my childhood home and made up my yard. Larger now and more majestic, they seem to have a greater story to tell. I can still see the remnants of the tree fort my brothers and I built in one of the large elm trees—back when we didn't know how to build a tree fort and we didn't care. It was sparse and childishly creative!

As I drive around through the excavation, I notice a home on the other side of the grove of trees. It is lifted up off the ground and sitting on steel beams made into a trailer. It rests between the grove of trees and the mowed barley field. As I look closer, I recognize it as the home I grew up in! (Apparently, it is going to be relocated.) Whoever is doing the work has taken great care to lift the home off its foundation and move it instead of just demolishing it.

As I park the car and walk over to the house, a swell of emotion comes over me. So many memories come rushing back into my being—not just in my mind but also in my cells, memories that have lain dormant for many years; they are sweet and very comforting. The memories of playing in the yard around the house with my brothers and sister, memories of playing with our dogs, two furry Samoyeds, memories of coming home each day and walking up the steps and feeling safe at home. Next come memories of my mother who has passed away. She was always there when we came home. Always there to care for us. Everything is different now, I think to myself, fully realizing the truth in the saying that you can never truly go home. The house is gone from its basement foundation. It has been uprooted like a tree from the soil. I know it is silly to feel upset about the home being moved, but I do anyway, and in some small and maybe wrong way, I can't help it. I feel a little violated somehow.

I walk to the front door of the house. I can't really call it a home anymore like I did growing up. There is no front porch. It just sits on large steel beams. Hanging three feet above the ground is the threshold of the front door I had crossed many times a day for over thirteen years from the time I was six to the time I was nineteen years old. When I reach up, to my surprise, I find the door unlocked. I open it and lift myself up inside.

I can hardly believe how small it is. I don't remember it being this small. How did my parents raise four children in such a small space? I smile, full of amazement, wonder, and fond memories. In my mind, I can picture the way it was when I was growing up, the way my mother and father took such fond care of it. They never owned the home. They had rented it all those years. Yet they had treated it as if it were theirs. I recall the pictures that were on the walls, the simple furniture we owned, the proud and sturdy oak dining table my father built that was too big for the room, but special to all of us.

When I walk into the kitchen, again, I am shocked by how small it is and yet how huge the memories are. So much love came out of this kitchen. My mother nurtured her family so well from this little room.

The two bedrooms seem small compared to what I remember. I walk in one and remember accidentally shooting a big hole in the wall with my father's rifle. I remember my father and mother with their arms around me—holding me and making sure I am all right after that careless mistake. A tear drips off my lower eyelid and onto the dusty floor.

I walk into the bathroom. It is so tiny. I laugh, remembering how we waited outside the door for someone else in the family to finish in the bathroom. I remember not wanting to wait for my sister or mother at times, and how several times I ran outside and peed in the bushes around the back of the house because I just couldn't wait any longer. As I look around one last time while standing by the front door, I take in a deep breath, as if to soak in as much as I can. I know I will never see it again, and strangely, somehow that is okay. I've been fortunate to see it here on this visit. It could have easily been moved already.

I hold back tears as I climb down, close the door, and walk away. I drive away with my mind a kaleidoscope of thoughts. How different my life is now. How different my children's lives are now. How much things change. Who I am is in part because of how I grew up. How hard my parents worked for so little. But I don't really remember ever feeling badly because we didn't have more. Yet we had plenty of friends who did. It wasn't as if we were not aware that there was more in the world around us. Just on the other side of Dry Creek, we had friends with homes that had family rooms as large as that entire house I'd just walked through. Their garages were twice the size of my home. My appreciation for my parents expands even more inside me, and I smile as I think of how much they taught me.

As I drive away, I look off to the right. Behind my view of the trees that line Dry Creek I notice the foothills in the distance. Instantly, my mind floods with the memories of Lost Canyon. I look at the clock in the car and realize I still have some time to drive out and see the canyon I haven't seen since my senior year of high school. The anticipation builds in me as I turn onto North Eagle Road and head north toward the amber brown foothills.

The road is paved much further than I remember. I am driving a very nice vehicle with air conditioning, unlike my first trip to the canyon. The ride is smooth and no dust is coming in through the vents or open windows. Again, a thought of how much things have changed quickly darts in and out of my mind.

As I pass the first big landmark, a small open valley with a steep hill on the south end, I remember how people would attempt to ride motorcycles up this steep hill. We called it "The Face." I remember how fun I thought this area was when I was younger. The asphalt road ends as my tires drop off the pavement and onto the gravel. I continue on the gravel road for a few more miles. As I drive down into the next little valley, I pull off the road and onto the turnoff to the canyon. As I pull off the main dirt road onto this side road I've been on many times before when I was younger, it feels the same, and yet somehow very different.

About fifty yards off the main road is a barbed wire livestock fence. It was always there before. At least I think I remember it. What is different is the big steel gate that now crosses the road where I want to go. It is clearly locked with a chain and padlock. There is a sign on the gate that says, "No Trespassing." There are more of these signs along the fence to the right and to the left, obviously to make it clear that someone doesn't want anyone behind the fence. I pull up to the gate, park the car, and turn off the engine. I sit for a while staring at the "No Trespassing" sign with my hands on the steering wheel. A sad feeling stirs in my heart with nowhere to go. I came all the way out here, but I can't get into one of my favorite places from childhood, a place I was eager to see again. "How dare they keep these memories from me," I think to myself as I climb out of the car and double check the lock on the gate—just in case. I again feel a little violated, the same strange feeling I experienced when walking up to my childhood home that had been uprooted.

I have no real right to feel this way—violated and wronged. It isn't really my canyon, but I always felt like it was. I climb back in the car and heave a sigh of resolved disgust. I guess that is it. I'm not ever going to return to my canyon. I will probably never see it again.

Later that night, I turn on my computer and log onto Google Earth. I can't just give up on finding Lost Canyon. I decide to try and locate it on satellite aerial photography. For over an hour I try to find it, but for some strange reason, I don't. It remains a frustrating mystery for me. I finally give up and go to bed. As I lie in bed, I can't sleep because I'm reflecting on the memories I have of the canyon and the times I spent there. How strange it is that I can't even find it on satellite photography. I wonder, in a silly way, whether it even existed in the first place. The doubt says to me, 'Maybe it has always been a figment of your imagination.' I laugh sadly to myself, knowing that memories this clear and vivid must be real.

Since I am spending the weekend with my father, I decide to share this experience with him when I wake in the morning. I want to see what he knows about the canyon. At breakfast, I ask him, "When was the last time you visited Lost Canyon?"

"It's been years," he says. I tell him my experience of not being able to find the canyon. He gets a puzzled look on his face and says, "Well, I can bet it didn't go anywhere." He doesn't know what to tell me though; he thinks I can still get there and tells me I was probably looking in the wrong place.

Later that day, a friend says that he thinks all that property, including the canyon, was purchased and the new owner fenced it all off from the public. I remember the "No Trespassing" sign.

I am sad that someone would block me from visiting the canyon. The memories I have of the canyon are bright and beautiful. They are so crisp that I can see the entire canyon in my mind. I can imagine each part of the canyon, and I can remember things that happened there—when I visited it as a boy with my father and as a young adult when I went with my friends—as if it were yesterday. I can even remember the smells in the different seasons, the sagebrush smells, and the different flowers in the spring. I can feel the heat of the rocks from the sun warming them all day as I sat on them and climbed on and around them. I can feel the coolness of the moss in the shade. I can see the mustard-colored lichen on the walls of the canyon, and I can hear the hawk overhead as it screams its greeting. I can feel the warm breeze as it rises up the canyon wall and caresses me as I stand on the side and look down into the open expanse.

My heart swells as I think of my lost son. Like the canyon I can't see or find, I can't see my son, but I realize I don't need to go back to the canyon because my memories are vivid. I can also live without my son, while I have to, because my memories of him are wonderful, and the more I focus on how grateful I am for the time I was blessed to share with him, the closer he is to me, and the closer I am to him.

---

# FINDING LOST CANYON

The next day I rethink my last attempt to find Lost Canyon. Maybe I didn't go far enough. Maybe I stopped at the wrong road. Maybe I ought to go back, go further down the main road, and see whether there's another access point that I've forgotten about.

As I pass the road with the gate, the "No Trespassing" sign makes me think about how sometimes in life we place "No Trespassing" signs on our memories. Further down the road, I come to another turnoff in the next valley over. It looks very similar to the one with the "No Trespassing" signs. It also has a gate that is locked, but just to its left is an entrance for foot traffic and horseback riders to pass through. I pull up and park my car. There is a large horse trailer parked next to the opening and a lady is grooming her horse. It looks to me as though she has just finished a long ride and is putting her horse and gear away.

I ask her whether she knows about "my" canyon. I tell her I grew up in the area and it has been years since I've been back, so I can't remember how to get there. She smiles a very satisfied smile and says, "Oh, I love that canyon. It's one of my favorite places to ride to. You can get there by driving if you go further on down the road to the next turnoff. There you will find another valley just like this one and another turn off that isn't gated."

"Thank you," I say with a satisfied smile and quickly leave.

My heart races with anticipation. Sure enough, there is another valley just over the hills and another turnoff just like the prior one. "I'm now going to find Lost Canyon," I shout in the car as I turn off the main road. I drive up a narrow valley. On both sides of me, the light breeze is caressing the dry grasses, causing what appear to be waves rolling across the hills. The light reflects off the grass differently as it bends and stands in the wind, reflecting gold, then bronze, back to my eyes as the waves roll along the hills.

As I crest the hill, my heart leaps with excitement. I am looking down at the canyon I haven't seen for years. There it is before me as grand as ever—just where I left it. I drive right to the spot my father stopped at that very first day we pulled up to the canyon as little children. I climb out and feel the warm breeze caress my face, just like before. The smells are just like I remembered them. And guess what is above me in the sky? The screech of a hawk calls out a greeting to me as he hangs in the breeze above me as if to say welcome back.

As I stand there, looking out over the memorable canyon of my childhood, I think of my other Canyon, my most important Canyon, the precious son I lost. I imagine him here next to me, looking out over this inspiring rock wonderland. I wish I could show it to him as my dad showed it to me. Unfortunately, I won't be able to do this today.

Yet, as I stand there, looking out over the canyon's edge, a tear runs down my cheek as I feel a strong impression that Canyon is already with me. He knows I love him. Like the little water bugs in the story I had once told Kevin, I long to know where my loved one has gone. Like the dragonfly, I believe Canyon is waiting patiently for us on the other side. And just like I have finally found Lost Canyon, I know I will also one day be with my son. Someday, I will pass through that silent door too, and when I do, I will tell him all the things I've been longing to say all these years, and he'll say, "I know, Dad."

Until then, I wait patiently and enjoy every minute of the time I have with the rest of my precious family. Until that day when I meet him on distant shore, I will do all I can to be a better man, father, husband, and friend. I know that is what Canyon would want. He would want me to focus on the things that matter most. He would want me to focus on what I have, rather than my loss. He would want me to celebrate him by celebrating the life I have.

# ABOUT THE AUTHOR

Sean Fleming is an adventure enthusiast with a passion for life. He has traveled the world and enjoys an active life. Sean has spent nearly twenty years in commercial real estate and land development. When not working, Fleming enjoys family time, travel, fly fishing, boating, snow skiing, snowboarding, and mountain biking. Fleming recently completed The Mongol Rally, a charity event in which he drove from London to Ulaanbaatar, Mongolia (more than 7,300 miles) in 26 days. An avid volunteer, Fleming devotes time to his church and community. A resident of Salt Lake City, Utah, Fleming is married and has five children.